Practical
Spiritual
Growth

Wole Olarinmoye

Be blessed as you read

Wole & Jarmu

Nov 17.

Practical Spiritual Growth

Wole Olarinmoye

Word2Print

A Division of One-Touch Pro Ltd

PRACTICAL SPRITUAL GROWTH

First published in the United Kingdom in 2017 by Word2Print
www.word2print.com
ISBN: 9781908588210

A CIP catalogue record for this title is available from the British Library

Edit: Karis Kolawole & Muyiwa Olumoroti

Cover design: Adeola Disu
The Kingdom Publications

Book design: Supreme Core Media
www.supremecoremedia.com

Printed and bound by
CPI Group (UK) Ltd,
Croydon, CR0 4YY

CONTENTS

SECTION 1: THE GOALS OF SPIRITUAL GROWTH

SECTION 2: THE GROWTH PROCESS FOR SPIRITUAL GROWTH

SECTION 3: THE GATEWAY TO SPIRITUAL GROWTH

SECTION 4: THE GEOLOGY OF SPIRITUAL GROWTH

CONCLUSION

PRACTICAL SPIRITUAL GROWTH

Introduction

Spiritual growth has been mystified by many clerics down the ages. Many people want to be close to God but are not keen on the religious set ups that obtain in most religious institutions. It is not uncommon to hear people talk about being spiritual but not religious and I wholeheartedly accept that. So how can we grow spiritually without being religious?

I am very passionate about this topic for a couple of reasons:

1. I have discovered that many people find it challenging to cross the boundaries of spiritual development. In many churches you find the 'spiritual children' and then the so called 'spiritually mature' and it's not often you see people crossing from children to becoming mature.

2. There is a big difference between being mature and not being mature. I have had the opportunity of being a Christian before I understood the word of God and I am now a Christian with understanding. I was a Christian before receiving the infilling of the Holy Spirit and after. I have been a Christian before a strong prayer life and after. I know what I had to do to cross the line from being a spiritual child to becoming a mature/maturing Christian and in this book I would like to share and explore with you how to grow spiritually in a practical non-religious way.

I wish you every blessing as you read in Jesus name.

Wole Olarinmoye

London UK

ACKNOWLEDGEMENTS

We thank the Lord for the wisdom, desire and ability to write this book. Lord, without You we would not have been able to do this. Thank You.

I must also thank my sweetheart, the love of my life, my best friend, confidant, cheerleader, encourager, prayer partner and woman of God, Dami Olarinmoye. I love you Honey!

A massive thank you to Dr Muyiwa Olumoroti, our publisher, whose attention to detail and commitment to excellence is really stressful! The finished work speaks for itself. My brother, for all the pain you keep putting me through to ensure we deliver something worth putting our name to, thank you!

A big thanks also to our editor and friend, the tender hearted, sweet spirited, undeniably gifted, Karis Kayode Kolawole whose invaluable contributions have made this book the success story that it is. The Lord bless you real good.

Special thanks also go to Pastor Allan Davies, Dr Taiwo Adewumi and Pastors Olus and Lola Awobowale for their contributions and doctrinal insights. The Lord grant you all grace to fulfil your ministry as you have helped me fulfil mine.

Finally, I want to acknowledge and thank God for the house of New Wine Church led by the senior minister Pastor Michael Olawore, where I have been planted for over 15 years. May the geology of this beloved house, continue to help men and women to discover, develop and deploy their gifts in Jesus name. God bless you all!

DEDICATION

This book is dedicated to Dr Tayo Adeyemi, founding pastor of New Wine Church, London. His mandate from God was to help people discover, develop and deploy their gifts. He exemplified this by recognising the grace on me, allowing me to teach a series on spiritual growth in 2009. Some of the material in this book is from that series. In 2011, while teaching on a message titled 'Be fruitful', he said, "Write a book and put your name on it." This is the third book with my name on it and I am not done yet. Your memory is ever blessed.

THE GOALS OF SPIRITUAL GROWTH

Ephesians 4:11-16

Now these are the gifts Christ gave to the church: the apostles, the prophets, the evangelists, and the pastors and teachers. 12 Their responsibility is to equip God's people to do his work and build up the church, the body of Christ. 13 This will continue until we all come to such unity in our faith and knowledge of God's Son that we will be mature in the Lord, measuring up to the full and complete standard of Christ.

14 Then we will no longer be immature like children. We won't be tossed and blown about by every wind of new teaching. We will not be influenced when people try to trick us with lies so clever they sound like the truth. 15 Instead, we will speak the truth in love, growing in every way more and more like Christ, who is the head of his body, the church. 16 He makes the whole body fit together perfectly. As each part does its own special work, it helps the other parts grow, so that the whole body is healthy and growing and full of love.

Ephesians 4:11-16

Now these are the gifts Christ gave to the church: the apostles, the prophets, the evangelists, and the pastors and teachers. 12 Their responsibility is to equip God's people to do his work and build up the church, the body of Christ. 13 This will continue until we all come to such unity in our faith and knowledge of God's Son that we will be mature in the Lord, measuring up to the full and complete standard of Christ.

14 Then we will no longer be immature like children. We won't be tossed and blown about by every wind of new teaching. We will not be influenced when people try to trick us with lies so clever they sound like the truth. 15 Instead, we will speak the truth in love, growing in every way more and more like Christ, who is the head of his body, the church. 16 He makes the whole body fit together perfectly. As each part does its own special work, it helps the other parts grow, so that the whole body is healthy and growing and full of love.

The Bible says that God has set in the body the five-fold ministry gifts for two reasons.

- Equipping
- Building

This will continue until we all come. The Amplified

version of the Bible says 'till we all attain and the New International Version says till we all reach'.

God wants us to reach, to attain and to come up to certain levels in our spiritual growth.

We are not supposed to be stagnant in our growth as believers. God expects us to keep growing until we attain. We are supposed to keep pressing towards.

Paul said in Philippians 3:12-13:

I don't mean to say that I have already achieved these things or that I have already reached perfection. But I press on to possess that perfection for which Christ Jesus first possessed me.

Spiritual growth is not a state or a place but a process.

However, growth and development must have a direction and a focus and the scripture we read in Ephesians chapter 4:11-16 holds what I call the seven goals of Spiritual Growth.

They are:

- Unity of the faith v13
- Knowledge of God's Son v13
- Mature in the Lord v13
- Standard of Christ v13
- No longer children in doctrine v14
- Speaking the truth in love v15
- Find your place, release your grace v16

These seven goals are the seven areas we must grow in as Christians. Growth in one area is good but not good enough. To be a well-rounded and established believer, we should see growth across all seven areas. We will discuss each one in turn to help us understand exactly what they mean and why they are goals of spiritual growth.

GOAL 1: UNITY OF THE FAITH

What does this mean?

The word unity means harmony, combining different things to be one. It also means to be in agreement. The word faith here comes from the Greek word 'pistis' which means conviction or persuasion. Those of us who share the conviction or persuasion of the Lordship of Jesus need to be in harmony and agreement. One of the main things the non-believing world has against us as Christians is the apparent lack of unity.

Why is it a goal of spiritual growth?

ONE: JESUS PRAYED FOR IT.

John 17:9-11, 20-23 says:

9 "My prayer is not for the world, but for those you have given me, because they belong to you. 10 All who are mine belong to you, and you have given them to me, so they bring me glory. 11 Now I am departing from the world; they are staying in this world, but I am coming to you. Holy Father, you have given me your name; now protect them by the power of your name so that they will be united just as we are.

20 "I am praying not only for these disciples but also for all who will ever believe in me through their message. 21 I pray that they will all be one, just as you and I are one—as you are in me, Father, and I am in you. And may they be in us so that the world will believe you sent me. 22 "I have given them the glory you gave me, so they may be one as we are one. 23 I am in them and you are in me. May they experience such perfect unity that the world will know that you sent me and that you love them as much as you love me.

If Jesus was so passionate about this concept of unity, then it has to be important. He made it clear that through our oneness certain clear outcomes will occur as a result:

- The world will believe that Jesus was sent of God (v20)
- The world will know that Jesus was sent of God (v23)

From this we can conclude that disunity and lack of agreement in the church is hampering the spread of the gospel. If the world does not believe or know that Jesus was sent of God, then we are not walking in the agreement and unity that Jesus expects. If Jesus was so hung up on agreement and unity, then it is crucial that we are in one accord so that we can see the outcomes He clearly identified.

TWO: THE DISCIPLES PRACTICED UNITY WITH ASTOUNDING RESULTS.

We often complain about the lack of the miraculous power of God in our midst today. One of the reasons the apostles enjoyed it so much was they walked in unity. The Bible says they testified POWERFULLY to the resurrection of Jesus. Their unity generated astounding results.

In Acts 1:14

they were united in prayer. They all met together and were constantly united in prayer, along with Mary the mother of Jesus, several other women, and the brothers of Jesus.

In Acts 4:32-33

As they continued in unity look at what happens; there was a release of God's power just because they were in agreement.

All the believers were united in heart and mind. And they felt that what they owned was not their own, so they shared everything they had. 33 The apostles testified powerfully to the resurrection of the Lord Jesus, and God's great blessing was upon them all.

Furthermore, God's blessing was upon ALL of them. For the church to have the same results, it is critical that we walk in the unity of the faith.

THREE: GOD HONOURS AND RESPECTS UNITY AND AGREEMENT OF ANY KIND.

So great is the power of unity and agreement that God Himself noted that being in unity and agreement more or less equated to having the ability to do the impossible. If mere men can potentially do the impossible if they are united, then how much more would the children of God be able to accomplish, if they are in agreement.

Genesis 11:5-6 says:

But the Lord came down to look at the city and the tower the people were building. 6 "Look!" he said. "The people are united, and they all speak the same language. After this, nothing they set out to do will be impossible for them!

This scripture tells us in no uncertain terms that God honours unity of any kind. If God had to intervene to disrupt the unity of unbelieving idol worshiping men whose prayers are an abomination to the Lord, then as a church we are missing out on a whole lot of miraculous power because of our lack of unity.

FOUR: PAUL DESCRIBED DIVISION AND SECTARIANISM AS INFANTHOOD.

1 Corinthians 3:1-4 says

Dear brothers and sisters, when I was with you I couldn't talk to you as I would to spiritual people. I had to talk as though you belonged to this world or as though you were infants in Christ. 2 I had to feed you with milk, not with solid food, because you weren't ready for

*anything stronger. And you still aren't ready,
3 for you are still controlled by your sinful
nature. You are jealous of one another and
quarrel with each other. Doesn't that prove
you are controlled by your sinful nature?
Aren't you living like people of the world? 4
When one of you says, "I am a follower of
Paul," and another says, "I follow Apollos,"
aren't you acting just like people of the world?*

This passage brings up a number of interesting points with reference to unity and spiritual growth.

If division and sectarianism are described as being tantamount to infanthood in Christ then by inference, unity and agreement would equate to being mature. Thus, allowing our various denominations to interfere with our Christian unity is immature according to the Bible. Paul in this passage makes it clear that holding on to being a follower of X, Y or Z is immaturity. We should be promoting the fact that we are followers of Christ and we belong to Him. That does not invalidate denominations by any means. Varied denominations mean we will all find an expression of worship that suits us. However, whatever denominational expression of Christ we choose to embrace, we should never forget in word or deed that we are collectively the Lords; even if the other person does not quite believe exactly as we do. We are not better or superior, less or inferior because of where or how we worship. We are all one in the Lord Jesus and our focus should be on Him.

Jealousy and quarrelling are signs of immaturity

according to the Bible. Unfortunately, we see a lot of this in the church. We find people jostling for attention and the end result is jealousy and insecurity. Others quarrel over differences of opinion. The Bible tells us both groups are immature.

You cannot be in unity alone. Therefore, anyone who tells you they don't need to be part of a church to be a Christian may be right in principle but also immature as this goal of spiritual growth aims to increase unity and fellowship in the body of Christ. (See Hebrews 10:25).

- If we have problems agreeing with other Bible believing Christians, then we need to grow in the unity of the faith.

- If you are in constant conflict with other believers, then you need to grow in the unity of the faith.

- If you have a problem respecting the differences of opinion of other Bible believing churches, then you need to grow in the unity of the faith.

GOAL 2: KNOWLEDGE OF GOD'S SON

What does this mean?

To help us understand this more we need to ask ourselves, who is the Son of God and what did He come to do?

Jesus is the Son of God and the gospels were written to make this clear to us. To fully explain who Jesus is would mean copying and pasting the whole New Testament in here. The first chapter of John's gospel is a good one to read but the first twelve verses give us some insight into who Jesus is.

> *In the beginning the Word already existed. The Word was with God, and the Word was God. 2 He existed in the beginning with God. 3 God created everything through him, and nothing was created except through him. 4 The Word gave life to everything that was created, and his life brought light to everyone. 5 The light shines in the darkness, and the darkness can never extinguish it. 6 God sent a man, John the Baptist, 7 to tell about the light so that everyone might believe because of his testimony. 8 John himself was not the light; he was simply a witness to tell about the light. 9 The one who is the true light, who gives light to everyone, was coming into the world. 10 He came into the very world he created, but the world didn't recognize him. 11 He came to his*

11

own people, and even they rejected him. 12 But to all who believed him and accepted him, he gave the right to become children of God.

Jesus Himself said in John 14:6:

Jesus told him, "I am the way, the truth, and the life. No one can come to the Father except through me.

Jesus is the Saviour of the world who came to die for us.

Romans 5:8 tells us:

But God showed his great love for us by sending Christ to die for us while we were still sinners.

So we can see who He is and what He came to do. However, He did not only come to save us from our sins; and this is where this chapter comes in, He came to do a lot more than that.

1 John 3:8b says:

But the Son of God came to destroy the works of the devil

I like the way the NKJV puts it:

For this purpose, the Son of God was manifested, that He might destroy the works of the devil.

What are the works of the devil?

John 10:10 quoting Jesus says:

The thief's purpose (talking about the devil) is to steal and kill and destroy. My (Jesus) purpose is to give them a rich and satisfying life.

So any form of sin, sickness, poverty or oppression is a work of the devil. These works of the devil have the potential to steal our peace and joy, kill and destroy our lives and purpose if left unchecked and unaddressed. Jesus came to destroy every single one of these works of the devil and give us a rich and satisfying life.

2 Peter 1: 3-4 says:

By his divine power, God has given us everything we need for living a godly life. We have received all of this by coming to know him, the one who called us to himself by means of his marvellous glory and excellence. 4 And because of his glory and excellence, he has given us great and precious promises. These are the promises that enable you to share his divine nature and escape the world's corruption caused by human desires.

Essentially this scripture explains that by knowing Jesus and by His divine power, we have everything we need for a godly life, everything we need to fulfil our existence here on earth.

Romans 8:31-32 says:

What shall we say about such wonderful things as these? If God is for us, who can ever be against us? 32 Since he did not spare even

his own Son but gave him up for us all, won't
he also give us everything else?

Having given us Jesus, God is willing to give us
EVERYTHING ELSE!

So what do we understand from all these scriptures?

- The Son of God came to save us from our sins and bring us closer to God
- The Son of God came to destroy the works of the devil.
- The Son of God came to give us a rich and satisfying life.
- The Son of God came to empower and equip us with the knowledge to live a godly life. In other words, He came to enable us to live a god-like life here on earth.
- The Son of God's sacrifice included everything else we need in this life.

In summary, having the knowledge of the Son of God, is to understand what Jesus came to do for you as an individual and how to walk in the experience of it.

Why is it a goal of spiritual growth?

ONE: GOD WANTS US TO PROSPER AND BE IN HEALTH

3 John 2 says:

Dear friend, I hope all is well with you and that you are as healthy in body as you are strong in spirit.

The apostle was writing to the disciples at the time and to us by inference hoping that all is well with us and that we are in health. We can deduce that God wants us to enjoy our lives and to be healthy and there are several scriptures that support this in addition to the ones above which show that Jesus came to destroy the works of the devil and to provide us with a rich satisfying life. This is further confirmed by 1 Peter 2:24b which says:

..by whose stripes you were healed.

The following scriptures show us that health, wealth and peace of mind are all promises we have been given but we will only be able to access them through knowing the Son of God and what He has done for us.

1 Timothy 6:17

Teach those who are rich in this world not to be proud and not to trust in their money, which is so unreliable. Their trust should be in God, who richly gives us all we need for our enjoyment.

2 Corinthians 8:9

You know the generous grace of our Lord Jesus Christ. Though he was rich, yet for your sakes he became poor, so that by his poverty he could make you rich.

2 Corinthians 9:8

And God will generously provide all you need. Then you will always have everything you need and plenty left over to share with others

Philippians 4:6-7

Don't worry about anything; instead, pray about everything. Tell God what you need, and thank him for all he has done. 7 Then you will experience God's peace, which exceeds anything we can understand. His peace will guard your hearts and minds as you live in Christ Jesus

TWO: NO MATTER HOW ANOINTED OR GIFTED YOU ARE, SIN, SICKNESS AND SATANIC OPPRESSION WILL LIMIT THE FULL OPERATION AND EXPRESSION OF GOD IN YOUR LIFE.

We need to increase in the knowledge of our rights in Him. Our service for God is extremely important but the Bible also says, *"My people are destroyed for lack of knowledge"*, *(Hosea 4:6 NKJV)*. If we have insufficient knowledge of what belongs to us by virtue of our relationship with the Son of God, then we risk being taken advantage of by the devil. This will severely limit our effectiveness in fulfilling the mandate of God for our lives.

In the Son of God, we have victory over the works of the devil. If there is anything that can be categorised as a work of the devil in our lives, we should grow to the point of having victory over it.

I started out on the path of faith after getting a revelation of Psalm 27:13. It says:

Yet I am confident I will see the Lord's goodness,
while I am here in the land of the living

That made me realise that God wanted us to enjoy His goodness while we were here in the land of the living BEFORE we get to Heaven! God's goodness includes health, wealth and the abundant life. So I started to exercise my faith more and more, standing on the promises of God's word and gradually by His grace, I started to enjoy more and more of all that He has already made available to us.

- If Jesus came to destroy sickness and we are still having struggles with ill health, then we need to grow in the knowledge of the Son of God.

- If Jesus came to destroy the works of the devil and we are still having struggles with various forms of oppression such as nightmares, unexplained negative occurrences which keep repeating themselves, then we need to grow in the knowledge of the Son of God.

- If Jesus became poor that we might be rich and we are still having struggles with poverty and debt, then we need to grow in the knowledge of the Son of God.

This aspect of spiritual growth deals with understanding our rights and privileges as believers and how to apply them.

GOAL 3: MATURE IN THE LORD

What does this mean?

The word mature means fully grown or fully developed. The NKJV uses the phrase 'Perfect man' instead of mature. The original word in the Bible translated as mature means to be complete in growth, mental and moral character. Thus being mature in the Lord refers to maturity in our Christian walk or growth, being fully grown or developed as believers. There are at least three aspects of maturity to explore:

ONE: MATURITY OF CHARACTER

Galatians 5:16-26

16 So I say, let the Holy Spirit guide your lives. Then you won't be doing what your sinful nature craves. 17 The sinful nature wants to do evil, which is just the opposite of what the Spirit wants. And the Spirit gives us desires that are the opposite of what the sinful nature desires. These two forces are constantly fighting each other, so you are not free to carry out your good intentions. 18 But when you are directed by the Spirit, you are not under obligation to the law of Moses. 19 When you follow the desires of your sinful nature, the results are very clear: sexual immorality, impurity, lustful pleasures, 20 idolatry, sorcery, hostility, quarrelling, jealousy, outbursts of anger, selfish ambition, dissension, division, 21 envy, drunkenness, wild parties, and other sins like these. Let me tell you again, as I have before, that anyone living that sort of life will not inherit the Kingdom of God. 22 But the Holy Spirit produces this kind of fruit in our lives: love, joy, peace, patience, kindness, goodness, faithfulness, 23 gentleness, and self-control. There is no law against these things! 24 Those who belong to Christ Jesus have nailed the passions and desires of their sinful nature to his cross and crucified them there. 25 Since we are living by the Spirit, let us follow the Spirit's leading in every part of our lives.26 Let us not become conceited, or provoke one another, or be jealous of one another.

I know you may have probably jumped the long passage above but please go back and read it fully and carefully. Reading the whole passage will bless you and help you to see the full expression of what we are discussing. To make it easier to understand, I will enumerate the specific points you should consider:

1. There are at least two of you-one that wants

to do evil (the flesh) and one that wants to do good (the spirit). The third part of you (the soul) decides who wins at each point in time. "Should I commit immorality?" The flesh says yes, the spirit says no. The mature soul will agree with the spirit, the immature soul will agree with the flesh. "Should I steal?" The flesh says yes, the spirit says no. The mature soul will agree with the spirit but the immature soul will agree with the flesh. You can extrapolate this for every situation.

2. Following the flesh has very clear outcomes listed in verses 19-21. Sin will limit you from fully enjoying all the Kingdom of God has to offer.

3. Following the Holy Spirit will result in you producing fruit (verses 16, 22-26). The fruit is the fully mature, fully developed part of a plant or tree. The fruit of the spirit, love, joy, peace, patience, kindness, goodness, faithfulness, gentleness, and self-control is the evidence of maturity of character.

Maturity of character can only be properly attained by the leading and guidance of the Holy Spirit, allowing Him to produce the fruit of spiritual maturity in you. We discuss this in more depth in the section on the gateway to spiritual growth.

TWO: MATURITY IN THE USE OF THE TONGUE

James 3:2.

*Indeed, we all make many mistakes. For if we
could control our tongues, we would be perfect
and could also control ourselves in every other
way.*

Another aspect of maturity in the Lord is maturity
in the use of your tongue. The scripture above
highlights the fact that we are human; we all make
mistakes but being able to control your tongue is
as close to perfection as it gets. Just the fact that
you are able to not offend people with your speech
or communication, i.e. what you say indicates you
have self-control.

THREE: MATURITY IN MANAGING ADVERSITY.

The devil's ultimate achievement is to break your
spirit. He delights in making you sin or sickly and
wants to oppress you but nothing makes him happier
than breaking the spirit of a believer. In fact, the sin,
sickness and oppression are merely tools to achieve
his ultimate aim of crushing your spirit, making
you question the sovereignty and integrity of God
(which is different from asking God questions),
bringing you to the place of losing faith and hope
in God. That's his ultimate goal. So if adversity is the
enemy's weapon or 'coup de grace' then a mature
believer must learn to endure adversity like Job did.
Even when he did not understand why his world

suddenly fell apart, he gave praise to God.

Job 1:20-22

20 Job stood up and tore his robe in grief. Then he shaved his head and fell to the ground to worship. 21 He said, "I came naked from my mother's womb, and I will be naked when I leave. The Lord gave me what I had, and the Lord has taken it away. Praise the name of the Lord!" 22 In all of this, Job did not sin by blaming God.

For context please feel free to read the whole of Job chapter 1.

He did not sin by blaming God. No wonder God described him in Job 1:1 as blameless.

There once was a man named Job who lived in the land of Uz. He was blameless—a man of complete integrity. He feared God and stayed away from evil.

A mature believer focuses on God in times of adversity. I once heard a saying: "If you cannot trace God, trust Him." James 5:10-11 says:

For examples of patience in suffering, dear brothers and sisters, look at the prophets who spoke in the name of the Lord. 11 We give great honour to those who endure under suffering. For instance, you know about Job, a man of great endurance. You can see how the Lord was kind to him at the end, for the Lord is full of tenderness and mercy.

James 1:3-4 also tells us that endurance is a mark of maturity and perfection in the Lord.

> *For you know that when your faith is tested, your endurance has a chance to grow. 4 So let it grow, for when your endurance is fully developed, you will be perfect and complete, needing nothing.*

Finally Proverbs 24:10 NKJV tells us that: *'If you faint in the day of adversity, your strength is small.'*

We are spiritually weak if we cannot withstand the pressures of adversity.

The problem with this aspect of Maturity in the Lord is that it does not come cheap. Most men and women of God in Bible times and even in the present day had to go through some tests of endurance which proved their maturity in the Lord.

So why is maturity in the Lord a goal of spiritual growth?

ONE: BEARING THE FRUIT OF THE SPIRIT IS A MARK OF GOOD, STRONG CHARACTER.

The Bible says just as you can identify a tree by its fruit, you can identify people by their actions (Matthew 7:20)

TWO: TONGUE CONTROL, AS WE HAVE SEEN, IS THE MARK OF PERFECTION. JOB DID NOT SIN IN HIS SPEECH.

THREE: IF YOU LOVE GOD WHEN THE GOING IS GOOD AND BAIL OUT WHEN THE GOING GETS TOUGH, YOU CANNOT BE TOO MATURE.

Paul said "I have learned how to cope in all situations, full or empty" (Philippians 4:12-13)

- If you are struggling with certain aspects of the fruit of the Spirit, then you need to grow in being mature in the Lord.
- If you are struggling with controlling your tongue and find yourself gossiping, backbiting, slandering and such like, then you need to grow in being mature in the Lord.
- If every time you face a challenging situation your faith in the Lord collapses, then you need to grow in being mature in the Lord.

GOAL 4: STANDARD OF CHRIST

What does this mean?

On the surface this would appear to be a repetition of the second one we looked at, the knowledge of the Son of God but this is looking at the full and complete Standard of Christ.

What does Christ mean? Christ from the original Greek means 'the Anointed One'. It means consecrated into an office. By His coming, Jesus was operating in an office, in a calling. It is the power of the Holy Spirit on Jesus that enabled Him to operate in His office as Christ. As Jesus, He is the Son of God who came to deliver us from the oppression of the devil and to provide us with a rich satisfying life. As the Christ, He is anointed and empowered to operate in His calling by the power of the Holy Spirit. Likewise, it is the power of the Holy Spirit on us as individuals that enables us to operate in whatever office or calling we have. If Jesus, embracing his humanity, depended on the Holy Spirit and His anointing, it is clear that we are to follow His example and do likewise.

So what is the full and complete Standard of Christ? The fullness of the power of the Holy Spirit on us to fulfil our calling. Look at how the Amplified version puts verse 13 of our foundation scripture.

> *Until we all reach oneness in the faith and in the knowledge of the Son of God, [growing spiritually] to become a mature believer, reaching to the measure of the fullness of Christ [manifesting His spiritual completeness and exercising our spiritual gifts in unity].*

The fullness of Christ is explained as manifesting His spiritual completeness and exercising our spiritual gifts in unity. I believe that we are all meant to grow into the fullness of the anointing (the Power of the Holy Spirit) that is available to us as individuals in our respective callings.

We are ALL called by God to do something specific for Him in this world. We are thus all anointed to fulfil that calling. Ephesians 4:7 says:

> However, he has given each one of us a special gift through the generosity of Christ.

This is further confirmed by 1 Corinthians 12:7
> A spiritual gift is given to each of us so we can help each other.

We have all been given spiritual gifts to help each other. One of my favourite scriptures is Ephesians 2:10 which says:

> For we are God's masterpiece. He has created us anew in Christ Jesus, so we can do the good things he planned for us long ago.

We are His masterpiece, put together and designed to fulfil His purpose.

For every calling there is an anointing (an equipping) and there are certain gifts of the Spirit or spiritual abilities that will enhance your calling. We are meant to grow into those gifts and become all we can be in the service of our Master. (The full and complete Standard of Christ).

We are not all going to be apostles, prophets, evangelists, pastors or teachers but we all fit somewhere and we all need to grow in the grace of what we are called to do. (See 1 Corinthians 12:27-31)

Having established that we all have callings,

this means we all need to grow in the anointing or the fullness of the Standard of Christ for us as individuals.

Growing in the Anointing of the Holy Spirit.

We are expected to grow in the anointing of the Holy Spirit. It is a mark of spiritual growth. It will involve a personal walk with the Holy Spirit to understand His calling on your life and the gifts and graces you need to fulfil that calling. You will need to spend time in prayer, studying the Word of God, reading books written by those who have gone ahead who have valuable experiences to share.

Having a pastor or a leader pray for you or anoint you with oil does not reduce the investment of time, study and dedication required to grow in the Anointing of the Holy Spirit. It is not a shortcut.

Sometimes the Lord will allow the impartation of a gift or grace when hands are laid on you by someone in the same line or calling as you but that does not remove the responsibility on you to seek God for yourself. See 1 Timothy 4:14 and 2 Timothy 1:6, in the Amplified version below.

Do not neglect the spiritual gift within you, [that special endowment] which was intentionally bestowed on you [by the Holy Spirit] through prophetic utterance when the elders laid their hands on you [at your ordination].

That is why I remind you to fan into flame

the gracious gift of God, [that inner fire—the special endowment] which is in you through the laying on of my hands [with those of the elders at your ordination].

Paul clearly told Timothy it is possible to have hands laid on you and the gift remains dormant and ineffective unless you activate it or fan it into flame. The prayer of a leader or the laying of hands does not reduce the investment of time and dedication required to grow in the anointing.

This is where some miss it in the church. Not every anointing is for you because we all have different callings. You need to grow in the anointing that is relevant for your calling. Many believers go for 'anointing services' or 'impartation services' in which someone who does not have your calling prays for you to impart you with 'the anointing'. That only leads to confusion as you are expected to grow in YOUR anointing which is relevant for YOUR calling.

The issue of the anointing and laying on of hands is a delicate one in the church today with lots of very extreme views. In the Old Testament, the use of the anointing oil was reserved for those who had a clear office (the King, the Prophet and the Priest). In the New Testament we are anointed directly by the Holy Spirit so there is not much place for the anointing oil except in ministering healing or deliverance. (Mark 6:13, James 5:14) These are the only two references in the New Testament where oil was used in prayer and both were for healing and/or deliverance. Even when leaders were being ordained, the elders simply laid hands on them, no oil was poured.

That does not make it wrong to anoint people with oil in this day and age but we should seek to be anointed directly by the Holy Spirit.

Why is this a goal of spiritual growth?

ONE: WE CANNOT BE EFFECTIVE IN OUR CALLING WITHOUT THE POWER AND ANOINTING OF THE HOLY SPIRIT.

Jesus said in Acts, wait till you are endued with power from on high. (Acts 1:8)

TWO: WE ARE ALL BUILDERS. (I CORINTHIANS 3:9-15). THE WORK WE BUILD DEPENDS ON HOW WELL WE ARE FUNCTIONING UNDER THE ANOINTING RATHER THAN ACCORDING TO OUR OWN WISDOM AND SKILL.

For completion let's look at Ephesians 3:16-20.

> *I pray that from his glorious, unlimited resources he will empower you with inner strength through his Spirit.17 Then Christ will make his home in your hearts as you trust in him. Your roots will grow down into God's love and keep you strong. 18 And may you have the power to understand, as all God's people should, how wide, how long, how high, and how deep his love is. 19 May you*

experience the love of Christ, though it is too great to understand fully. Then you will be made complete with all the fullness of life and power that comes from God. 20 Now all glory to God, who is able, through his mighty power at work within us, to accomplish infinitely more than we might ask or think.

There is only one way by which you will attain that level of anointing; by having the love of God. When we are operating in unity and are walking in the love that passes knowledge (in the realm of revelation) then we can enjoy the full and complete standard of Christ.

- If we are still struggling to understand the purpose and calling of God for our lives, then we need to grow in the Standard of Christ.

- If we do not feel we have the full range of spiritual equipment we need to fulfil our purpose, then we need to grow in the Standard of Christ

- If we are not actively walking and pursuing the fulfilment of purpose, then we need to grow in the Standard of Christ.

GOAL 5: NO LONGER CHILDREN

What does this mean?

This is Christian growth with specific reference to

understanding fundamental Christian doctrine. The Bible uses the phrase 'not being tossed by every wind of doctrine'. If you are fortunate to be planted in a good church then you can feel confident that most, if not all the teaching you hear is based on the word of God. But look again at what verse 14 from our foundation passage says.

> *Then we will no longer be immature like children. We won't be tossed and blown about by every wind of new teaching. We will not be influenced when people try to trick us with lies so clever they sound like the truth.*

If you are taught something that sounds like the word of God but isn't would you know the difference? A spiritual child is one who does not know the difference between good teaching and bad teaching. Unfortunately, the devil is always trying to deceive Christians by altering the truth in such a way that will be unrecognisable to the spiritual child.

Acts 17:11 tells us about a group of people from Berea:

> *10 That very night the believers sent Paul and Silas to Berea. When they arrived there, they went to the Jewish synagogue. 11 And the people of Berea were more open-minded than those in Thessalonica, and they listened eagerly to Paul's message. They searched the Scriptures day after day to see if Paul and Silas were teaching the truth.*

These Berean believers did what many Christians

today do not do. They searched the scriptures to verify that what the Apostle was teaching them was the truth. There was no way some bad teaching was going to get past them because they searched with a view to learn the truth not just accept whatever they were told. They wanted to learn but they wanted to be sure they were learning the right thing.

1 John 4:1 encourages us to test what we hear. *Dear friends, do not believe everyone who claims to speak by the Spirit. You must test them to see if the spirit they have comes from God. For there are many false prophets in the world*

Paul knew too well the deception we can be exposed to and spoke about it in 2 Corinthians 11:12-15:

12 But I will continue doing what I have always done. This will undercut those who are looking for an opportunity to boast that their work is just like ours. 13 These people are false apostles. They are deceitful workers who disguise themselves as apostles of Christ. 14 But I am not surprised! Even Satan disguises himself as an angel of light. 15 So it is no wonder that his servants also disguise themselves as servants of righteousness. In the end they will get the punishment their wicked deeds deserve.

Jesus also warned us of the impending danger of false teaching in Matthew 24:24-25.

24 For false messiahs and false prophets will rise up and perform great signs and wonders so as to deceive, if possible, even God's chosen ones. 25 See, I have warned you about this ahead of time.

We must all be careful to ensure we are not being deceived by false teaching. As growing believers, we must be able to distinguish between good teaching and bad teaching. I call it having a good spiritual digestive system. When you are fed good spiritual food, absorb it and use it to grow spiritually but when you are fed bad spiritual food, discard it and do not let it into your life.

In Acts 2:42-43 we see the evidence of what is called the apostles teaching:

All the believers devoted themselves to the apostles' teaching, and to fellowship, and to sharing in meals (including the Lord's Supper), and to prayer. 43 A deep sense of awe came over them all, and the apostles performed many miraculous signs and wonders.

What is lacking in many churches today? A deep sense of awe or reverence for God and miraculous signs and wonders. From Acts 2:42 we see that reverence and power in the early church was triggered by all the believers devoting themselves to the apostles teaching, along with walking in love (sharing and caring) and prayer.

So what is the apostles teaching?

Hebrews 5:12 up to Hebrews 6:2 gives us some insight into this.

> *12 You have been believers so long now that you ought to be teaching others. Instead, you need someone to teach again the basic things about God's word. You are like babies who need milk and cannot eat solid food. 13 For someone who lives on milk is still an infant and doesn't know how to do what is right.14 Solid food is for those who are mature, who through training have the skill to recognize the difference between right and wrong.*
>
> *So let us stop going over the basic teachings about Christ again and again. Let us go on instead and become mature in our understanding. Surely we don't need to start again with the fundamental importance of repenting from evil deeds and placing our faith in God. 2 You don't need further instruction about baptisms, the laying on of hands, the resurrection of the dead, and eternal judgment.*

This passage is loaded! Let me summarise what this is saying in a few points.

- We need to grow to the point where we all know and can teach the basic principles of God's word (Hebrews 5:12 and 6:1)
- We need to grow to the point or become

mature in our understanding such that we can recognise right teaching from wrong teaching (v14)

It then lists the basic teachings as:

- Repenting from evil deeds
- Faith in God
- Baptisms
- Laying on of hands
- Resurrection of the dead
- Eternal judgement.

If you do not know what the Bible says about the basic teachings stated above and cannot scripturally explain them, then you need to mature in this aspect of spiritual growth.

To help us, I will give a brief insight into these basic areas, but you may require more personal study to gain proper understanding.

(A) REPENTING FROM EVIL DEEDS:

As a basic teaching, this deals with why we should repent from evil deeds and the consequence of not doing so. Galatians 5:19-23 explains it clearly.

19 When you follow the desires of your sinful nature, the results are very clear: sexual immorality, impurity, lustful pleasures, 20 idolatry, sorcery, hostility, quarrelling, jealousy, outbursts of anger, selfish ambition, dissension, division, 21 envy, drunkenness, wild parties, and other sins like these. Let me tell you again, as I have before, that anyone living that sort of life will not inherit the Kingdom of God.

Romans 6:23

For the wages of sin is death, but the free gift of God is eternal life through Christ Jesus our Lord

Not repenting from evil deeds has consequences. We need to continuously live and grow in the life that Jesus has secured for us, delivering us from the hold and bondage of sin.

(B) FAITH IN GOD:

As a basic teaching, this deals with believing in God and learning to trust Him in all areas of our lives including believing Him to provide for all our needs. Hebrews 11:6 says,

And it is impossible to please God without faith. Anyone who wants to come to him must believe that God exists and that he rewards those who sincerely seek him.

Hebrews 10:38a

And my righteous ones will live by faith...

(C) BAPTISMS:

As a basic teaching, every believer should be familiar with the two types of baptism: water baptism and the Holy Spirit baptism.

Water baptism will not take you to Heaven but it is an ordinance established by Jesus to signify the death, burial and resurrection of Jesus. The believer is fully immersed in water (death and burial) and then brought out (raised). Both Jesus and Paul talk about the significance of water baptism.

In Matthew 28:18:

18 Jesus came and told his disciples, "I have been given all authority in heaven and on earth. 19 Therefore, go and make disciples of all the nations, baptizing them in the name of the Father and the Son and the Holy Spirit.

Paul the Apostle further explains its significance in Romans 6:1-6

Well then, should we keep on sinning so that God can show us more and more of his wonderful grace? 2 Of course not! Since we have died to sin, how can we continue to live in it? 3 Or have you forgotten that when we were joined with Christ Jesus in baptism, we joined him in his death?4 For we died and were buried with Christ by baptism. And just as Christ was raised from the dead by the glorious power of the Father, now we also may live new lives. 5 Since we have been united with him in his death, we will also be raised to life as he was. 6 We know that our old sinful selves were crucified with Christ so that sin might lose its power in our lives. We are no longer slaves to sin.

Water baptism reminds us that we are dead to sin and alive to God through Jesus Christ.

In John 14:26, John 15:26 and again in John 16:12-15, Jesus introduces the Holy Spirit and explains His role.

But when the Father sends the Advocate as my representative—that is, the Holy Spirit—he will teach you everything and will remind you of everything I have told you.

But I will send you the Advocate, the Spirit of truth. He will come to you from the Father and will testify all about me.

There is so much more I want to tell you, but you can't bear it now. 13 When the Spirit of truth comes, he will guide you into all truth. He will not speak on his own but will tell you what he has heard. He will tell you about the future.14 He will bring me glory by telling you whatever he receives from me. 15 All that belongs to the Father is mine; this is why I said, 'The Spirit will tell you whatever he receives from me.'

The word 'Advocate' has a much broader meaning

in the original Greek translation. It is the word 'Parakletos' meaning one called to walk along side. It conveys the meaning of a person who is a helper, comforter, advocate, intercessor, counsellor, strengthener and standby. In other words, the Holy Spirit is to us, what Jesus was to His disciples; the Holy Spirit is our own personal Jesus.

Furthermore, Acts 1:5,8 tells us that the Holy Spirit will empower us.

> *5 John baptized with water, but in just a few days you will be baptized with the Holy Spirit."*

> *8 But you will receive power when the Holy Spirit comes upon you. And you will be my witnesses, telling people about me everywhere—in Jerusalem, throughout Judea, in Samaria, and to the ends of the earth."*

From all these passages, we see Jesus explaining to us the role of the Holy Spirit.

- He will teach us everything we need to know. (John 14:26)
- He will remind us of what we have been taught.
- He will tell us more about Jesus. (John 15:26)
- He will guide us into all truth. (John 16:13)
- He will tell us about the future.
- He will convey to us what He receives from Jesus. (John 16:14)
- He will empower us to be witnesses. (Acts 1:8)

(D) LAYING ON OF HANDS:

In the Old Testament, hands were laid to commission certain people into specific offices. (The King, Prophet and Priest). Hands were laid on them by the Prophet of God or Priest and they were anointed with oil. The oil represented the anointing or power of the Holy Spirit as they did not have the baptism of the Holy Spirit as we do today.

In the New Testament, the laying of hands has a twofold purpose. The first is to commission leaders or ministers into an office as in the Old Testament. This is primarily symbolic as we are directly anointed by the Holy Spirit. The second is to minister healing and deliverance. When Paul the Apostle warns about not laying hands suddenly, he is referring mainly to the commissioning of people into leadership roles.

1 Timothy 5:22

Never be in a hurry about appointing a church leader. Do not share in the sins of others. Keep yourself pure.

The first part of this verse in the King James Version says: *Lay hands suddenly on no man..*

Associated with laying hands is anointing with oil but I have already explained about this under the heading Standard of Christ.

(E) RESURRECTION OF THE DEAD:

As a basic teaching, every believer should be familiar with the fact that we will all rise again. 1 Thessalonians 4:13-17 tells us:

> *And now, dear brothers and sisters, we want you to know what will happen to the believers who have died so you will not grieve like people who have no hope. For since we believe that Jesus died and was raised to life again, we also believe that when Jesus returns, God will bring back with him the believers who have died. We tell you this directly from the Lord: We who are still living when the Lord returns will not meet him ahead of those who have died. For the Lord himself will come down from heaven with a commanding shout, with the voice of the archangel, and with the trumpet call of God. First, the believers who have died will rise from their graves. Then, together with them, we who are still alive and remain on the earth will be caught up in the clouds to meet the Lord in the air. Then we will be with the Lord forever.*

Revelations 20:11-15

> *And I saw a great white throne and the one sitting on it. The earth and sky fled from his presence, but they found no place to hide. 12 I saw the dead, both great and small, standing before God's throne. And the books were opened, including the Book of Life. And the*

dead were judged according to what they had done, as recorded in the books.13 The sea gave up its dead, and death and the grave gave up their dead. And all were judged according to their deeds. 14 Then death and the grave were thrown into the lake of fire. This lake of fire is the second death. 15 And anyone whose name was not found recorded in the Book of Life was thrown into the lake of fire.

Everyone will rise again, believers to meet with the Lord and non-believers to meet with judgement. This brings us nicely to the final basic teaching of Eternal judgement.

(F) ETERNAL JUDGEMENT:

As a basic teaching, we should all know that we will all be judged according to our words and deeds. See Matthew 12:36 and Hebrews 9:27 below.

And I tell you this, you must give an account on judgment day for every idle word you speak.

And just as each person is destined to die once and after that comes judgement...

Romans 2:5-11 puts this in such a clear way that I will round up with this:

But because you are stubborn and refuse to turn from your sin, you are storing up terrible punishment for yourself. For a day of anger is coming, when God's righteous judgment will be revealed. 6 He will judge everyone according to what they have done. 7 He will give eternal life to those who keep on doing good, seeking after the glory and honour and immortality that God offers. 8 But he will pour out his anger and wrath on those who live for themselves, who refuse to obey the truth and instead live lives of wickedness. 9 There will be trouble and calamity for everyone who keeps on doing what is evil—for the Jew first and also for the Gentile. 10 But there will be glory and honour and peace from God for all who do good—for the Jew first and also for the Gentile. 11 For God does not show favouritism.

We started off with repentance from dead works as a basic teaching and the reason it is so important is that we will all face eternal judgment.

These are the basic teachings we should all be familiar with as believers.

Why is this a goal of spiritual growth?

ONE: WE MUST BE ABLE TO CLEARLY ARTICULATE WHAT WE BELIEVE OR WE WILL NOT RECOGNISE FALSE TEACHING WHEN IT COMES ALONG.

TWO: WE SHOULD MATURE TO THE POINT THAT WE CAN TEACH WHAT WE BELIEVE

TO OTHERS LESS MATURE IN FAITH.

I made up my mind to become doctrinally sound when I was in University. Some chaps were going from room to room preaching and when they noticed that I showed interest, I was invited to join a weekly bible study to help me grow. After the second week, my spirit felt uncomfortable with what I was being taught. Somehow I knew it was wrong, but I didn't know enough of the word of God to disprove it. I started to voraciously feed on the word of God. I noted and then studied every scripture they preached in context for clearer understanding. One day, I challenged him using the scriptures to back up what I was saying. That was the last time the bible study held in my room.

- If you cannot explain or teach the basic principles of the word of God, then you need to grow in this area.

- If you are not sure you can recognise false teaching if it comes your way, then you need to grow in this area.

- If you are not in the habit of verifying what you are taught by the scriptures (irrespective of who teaches it) then you need to grow in this area. (See Acts 17:10-11)

GOAL 6: SPEAKING THE TRUTH IN LOVE

What does this mean?

It means speaking the truth in love! It is not enough to speak the truth, a mature believer does it with love as his motivation. When do you usually need to speak the truth in love? When there is a disagreement, difference of opinion, dispute, correction, chastisement or conflict. You need to convey some information to someone, something possibly unpleasant, information which you feel is for their benefit. This aspect of spiritual growth deals with conflict management and resolution.

There are three operative words we will look at: speaking, truth and love. When trying to convey something of importance, attention must be given to these three operative words.

The speaking must be done clearly, in a language and manner the recipient can understand. Good communication involves effective speaking and effective listening.

It is important that whatever is conveyed should be the truth. The Bible warns clearly against spreading falsehood and lies. Be very aware that truth is a matter of perspective and opinion. It was Marcus Aurelius the great Roman general and leader who said:

Everything we hear is an opinion, not the fact.

What does this mean?

It means speaking the truth in love! It is not enough to speak the truth, a mature believer does it with love as his motivation. When do you usually need to speak the truth in love? When there is a disagreement, difference of opinion, dispute, correction, chastisement or conflict. You need to convey some information to someone, something possibly unpleasant, information which you feel is for their benefit. This aspect of spiritual growth deals with conflict management and resolution.

There are three operative words we will look at: speaking, truth and love. When trying to convey something of importance, attention must be given to these three operative words.

The speaking must be done clearly, in a language and manner the recipient can understand. Good communication involves effective speaking and effective listening.

It is important that whatever is conveyed should be the truth. The Bible warns clearly against spreading falsehood and lies. Be very aware that truth is a matter of perspective and opinion. It was Marcus Aurelius the great Roman general and leader who said:

> *Everything we hear is an opinion, not the fact.*
> *Everything we see is a perspective, not the truth.*

So be careful about conveying information you have heard or seen without taking proper steps to verify if it is indeed the whole truth or not. A half-truth can be equally as damaging a lie.

The most important of these 3 however is love as it can determine how the truth that has been spoken will be received. Love must be our motive in speaking and even in living as a whole. It is not enough to say or do what is right, it must be done with the right motive of love.

1 Corinthians 13, the great chapter on love has this to say from verse 1-3

> *If I could speak all the languages of earth and of angels, but didn't love others, I would only be a noisy gong or a clanging cymbal. 2 If I had the gift of prophecy, and if I understood all of God's secret plans and possessed all knowledge, and if I had such faith that I could move mountains, but didn't love others, I would be nothing. 3 If I gave everything I have to the poor and even sacrificed my body, I could boast about it; but if I didn't love others, I would have gained nothing.*

I could be gifted with natural and/or spiritual languages, inspired in my preaching and prophesy, have depth of understanding, faith to move mountains and selfless to the point of giving the ultimate sacrifice (my life) but if I do any or all of those things without love as my motive, I gain nothing.

There are several people all over the world serving in various capacities in churches, charities, communities, civic groups but if they serve without love as their motive, in spiritual terms they gain nothing in the sight of God. So what is this love that is so important? I will explain what this love is using the following passages

Colossians 3:17, 23-24

And whatever you do or say, do it as a representative of the Lord Jesus, giving thanks through him to God the Father.

23 Work willingly at whatever you do, as though you were working for the Lord rather than for people. 24 Remember that the Lord will give you an inheritance as your reward, and that the Master you are serving is Christ.

John 14:21

Those who accept my commandments and obey them are the ones who love me. And because they love me, my Father will love them. And I will love them and reveal myself to each of them."

When you say or do something primarily for the Lord's glory rather than for men, you are demonstrating the love of God.

When you speak to a person about an issue primarily because you want God to be glorified in that situation then you are speaking the truth in love.

When you correct someone who is doing wrong because you want God to be glorified and not because you want to be proven right, you are speaking the truth in love.

When you speak to your spouse about a fault or weakness primarily because you want him or her to be a better person thus glorifying God rather than you just wanting to be a nag or to hurt their feelings, then you are speaking the truth in love.

When you call a brother or sister who has wronged you to reconcile with them primarily because you want to glorify God in keeping His command to walk in love rather than to tell them 'home truths' then you are speaking the truth in love.

When you see someone deviating from the right way and you call them to order primarily because you want God to be glorified rather than to show your superiority then you are speaking the truth in love.

Speaking the truth in love thus means, not being judgemental, not condemning, not patronising, not trying to use age or position to convey your point but trying to transmit truth in a loving manner.

Why is speaking the truth in love a goal of spiritual growth?

ONE: HANDLING CONFLICT WRONGLY HAS LED TO THE BREAKDOWN OF MANY FRIENDSHIPS, RELATIONSHIPS AND MARRIAGES.

There is a scriptural way to handle conflict and its application is a goal of spiritual growth. See what Matthew 18:15-17 says

> 15 *"If another believer sins against you, go privately and point out the offense. If the other person listens and confesses it, you have won that person back. 16 But if you are unsuccessful, take one or two others with you and go back again, so that everything you say may be confirmed by two or three witnesses. 17 If the person still refuses to listen, take your case to the church. Then if he or she won't accept the church's decision, treat that person as a pagan or a corrupt tax collector.*

Unfortunately, we often see conflict either remain unresolved or Christians start peddling rumours about each other resulting in seeds of bitterness being sown. Bitterness is a cancer that destroys friendships, relationships, marriages and even churches from the inside. Hebrews 12: 15 explicitly explains:

> *Look after each other so that none of you fails to receive the grace of God. Watch out that no poisonous root of bitterness grows up to trouble you, corrupting many.*

TWO: CONFLICT MANAGEMENT AND
RESOLUTION IS A PRIORITY TO JESUS.

He said if while presenting your gift at the altar, you remember your brother has something against you, first reconcile before you give your gift. Matthew 5:23-24 says:

> 23 *"So if you are presenting a sacrifice at the altar in the Temple and you suddenly remember that someone has something against you, 24 leave your sacrifice there at the altar. Go and be reconciled to that person. Then come and offer your sacrifice to God.*

GOAL 7: FIND YOUR PLACE, RELEASE YOUR GRACE

This passage tells us that even when you have not done anything wrong, just the fact that someone else thinks you have, leave your gift at the altar and make attempts to reconcile. Apologising for doing wrong takes humility, but reconciling with your brother purely for the purpose of walking in love is a mark of Spiritual maturity.

Many years ago, my relationship with another brother became strained. It went on for a few weeks and started to become obvious as we served in the same group. By right, I could have sat on my high horse as the leader of the group expecting him to come and 'submit' to me. However, after a meeting one day, I walked up to him, opened up the matter and we resolved it there and then. I chose to take the high road and walk in love rather than continue with the strained relationship.

- If you always want to be right in arguments, irrespective of how it will make others feel, then you need to grow in this area.
- If love is not your motive in the things you say or do, then you need to grow in this area.
- If you find yourself hurting people with your words, either because you are rude or because you are condescending, then you need to grow in this area

What does this mean?

It means there is a place where you add the most value in the body of Christ by being who you were designed to be. When we all find our place and release our grace, the bible tells us in Ephesians 4:16 from our foundation passage that certain things will happen.

He makes the whole body fit together perfectly. As each part does its own special work, it helps the other parts grow, so that the whole body is healthy and growing and full of love.

- We will fit together perfectly.
- We will help other parts of the body of Christ grow
- The whole body of Christ will be healthy

- The whole body of Christ as a whole will be growing
- The body of Christ will be full of love

Ephesians 4:7 says:
However, he has given each one of us a special gift through the generosity of Christ

You were created, designed and set apart to do something special in a way and in a place no one else can. The whole body of Christ (not just your local church) is dependent on you finding your place and releasing your grace.

It is not enough to recognise you are part of a body. It is not enough to know how to get your victory or even to be a perfect man. It is not enough to have the anointing, be doctrinally sound and know how to resolve conflict, you also need to know how to find your place and release your own special grace. It is important that you find and settle in the place where you add the most value. This is what actually results in the whole body growing, when we all do our share and play our part.

Ephesians 2:10 explains to us how unique and special we are.

For we are God's masterpiece. He has created us anew in Christ Jesus, so we can do the good things he planned for us long ago.

I like that! Masterpiece! That's what we are, God's masterpiece; created and designed to do something specific, something special. There is something no one else can do like you, find it and do it and you will be releasing your grace in your special place. Only mature individuals in a household contribute productively, children mainly take and take.

Finding your place and releasing your grace involves knowing what to do, and where to do it. There are 206 bones in the adult human body and they all fit in a specific place. There are various organs and systems in the body all designed to do very different specific things. Medically speaking, when a part of the body leaves its place of assignment and starts to try thriving somewhere else, we call it cancer and we aim to destroy it as soon as possible. It is out of place and will only cause disruption and destruction. Unfortunately, there are many in the body of Christ who are either wrongly placed or doing the wrong things and they are causing cancer in the church.

This seventh goal essentially deals with the issue of purpose. In our flagship book, the Decasections of Life, we have a whole chapter dedicated to purpose which will bless you greatly. In that chapter, we explain that there are three elements of purpose, three questions you need to ask for reflection and introspection to help you in your journey to fulfilling purpose. They are:

- Who are you?
- What should you be doing?
- Where should you be?

If you don't have the book, you can access the chapter on purpose free on our website at www. decasections.org or woleolarinmoye.com

Why is this a goal of spiritual growth?

ONE: IT TAKES MATURITY TO KNOW SPECIFICALLY WHAT YOU SHOULD BE DOING IN THE BODY OF CHRIST.

When we start serving in the kingdom of God, we do whatever it is we are asked to do. With maturity you realise you have both a special grace and a special place where you are at your best for the Lord, and in life as whole. At this point you do what you are designed to do, where you are designed to do it.

TWO: IT TAKES MATURITY TO KNOW SPECIFICALLY WHERE YOU SHOULD BE LOCATED IN THE BODY OF CHRIST.

Just as you are not called to do everything, likewise you are not called to be everywhere. There is a place you add the most value and it takes maturity to stay there. I call this your Divine Location and you will learn more about this in the free chapter on Purpose from our book the Decasections of Life.

THE GROWTH PROCESS OF SPIRITUAL GROWTH

In section 1 we looked at the seven Goals of Spiritual Growth. They are:

- Unity of the faith
- Knowledge of God's Son
- Mature in the Lord
- Full and complete standard of Christ
- No longer children in doctrine
- Speaking the truth in love
- Find your place, release your grace

We explained that many people find it challenging to cross from one level of Spiritual Maturity to another so it is important to know and understand what the goals are.

We also explained that God has given the five-fold ministry gifts of apostle, prophet, evangelist, pastor and teacher for the purpose of equipping and building us till we reach, attain and grow into Spiritual Maturity.

In this section we must first establish that spiritual maturity is not a state or a place but an ongoing process which only ends when we see Him face to face.

If we say section 1 deals with where we are going (goals) then this section will help us to locate where we are in our spiritual growth.

If you are going somewhere using a map or a satellite navigation system, you need to locate where you are as well as where you are going to help you plot a course.

There are two ways to locate where you are spiritually. The first is the traditional way called Stages of Spiritual development, the second is Practical Spiritual Growth.

STAGES OF SPIRITUAL DEVELOPMENT

There are three stages of spiritual development broadly speaking. These are mentioned by Apostle John in 1 John 2:12-20:

I am writing to you who are God's children because your sins have been forgiven through Jesus. 13 I am writing to you who are mature in the faith because you know Christ, who existed from the beginning. I am writing to you who are young in the faith because you have won your battle with the evil one. 14 I have written to you who are God's children because you know the Father. I have written to you who are mature in the faith because you know Christ, who existed from the beginning.

I have written to you who are young in the faith because you are strong. God's word lives in your hearts, and you have won your battle with the evil one. 15 Do not love this world nor the things it offers you, for when you love the world, you do not have the love of the Father in you. 16 For the world offers only a craving for physical pleasure, a craving for everything we see, and pride in our achievements and possessions. These are not from the Father, but are from this world. 17 And this world is fading away, along with everything that people crave. But anyone who does what pleases God will live forever. 18 Dear children, the last hour is here. You have heard that the Antichrist is coming, and already many such antichrists have appeared. From this we know that the last hour has come. 19 These people left our churches, but they never really belonged with us; otherwise they would have stayed with us. When they left, it proved that they did not belong with us. 20 But you are not like that, for the Holy One has given you his Spirit, and all of you know the truth.

From the scriptures you can see that John refers to three categories of believers.
- Spiritual children
- Young in faith
- Mature in faith

We will look at these in turn.

SPIRITUAL CHILDREN

This refers to those at the starting point of spiritual growth. There is absolutely nothing wrong with being a child. The real issue is remaining a child for longer than is expected.

In Matthew 18:1-4, Jesus tells us there are some qualities of children we should never grow out of.

> *About that time the disciples came to Jesus and asked, "Who is greatest in the Kingdom of Heaven?" 2 Jesus called a little child to him and put the child among them. 3 Then he said, "I tell you the truth, unless you turn from your sins and become like little children, you will never get into the Kingdom of Heaven. 4 So anyone who becomes as humble as this little child is the greatest in the Kingdom of Heaven.*

Jesus clearly says that after turning from our sins we should become like little children! Isn't that interesting! Anyone who humbles himself as a little child is the greatest in the Kingdom of Heaven. So spiritual growth, becoming more mature spiritually, actually means becoming more like a child; more dependent on our Father and being more humble in our disposition.

There is nothing wrong with starting off as a child but remaining a spiritual child longer than is expected is delayed development. So what are the characteristics of a spiritual child? From 1 John 2 we see the following characteristics:

Spiritual children are still living in sin (verse 12).

This is why John writes to tell them their sins are forgiven. The sin issue has not been fully dealt with. There is not much difference in the life lived by them and that of an unbeliever. In verse 1 of the same 1 John 2, John says I am writing to you so that you will not sin. He goes on to explain in the following verses about Jesus being our advocate and that we cannot say we know God if we will not keep His commandments. Spiritual children still have an issue with obedience to the commandments of God. Hebrews 5:11-14 says:

> *There is much more we would like to say about this, but it is difficult to explain, especially since you are spiritually dull and don't seem to listen. 12 You have been believers so long now that you ought to be teaching others. Instead, you need someone to teach you again the basic things about God's word. You are like babies who need milk and cannot eat solid food. 13 For someone who lives on milk is still an infant and doesn't know how to do what is right. 14 Solid food is for those who are mature, who through training have the skill to recognize the difference between right and wrong.*

Here we see that Christians who should be teaching others but still need to be taught the basics are spiritual children.

Spiritual children know the Father (verse 14)

We should all know the Lord as our Heavenly Father but contrast that with the mature in faith who knows Christ (the Anointed One and His anointing). The relationship a spiritual child has with God is limited to little more than a 'give me, give me, give me' relationship. "What can God do for me? What can I get out of God? What's in this for me?" He has not matured to the place of "What can I do for God?" or "What can God do through me?"

Spiritual children are at risk of deception (verse 18)

John was warning about a group of people he referred to as antichrists. If you read further down to verse 26 you will see that essentially, antichrist is anyone who has the potential to lead people astray. Anyone who is preaching a gospel that is not properly centred on the word of God is classed as an antichrist. Unfortunately, spiritual children are at risk of being deceived by them due to their lack of grounding spiritually. This lack of grounding is due to insufficient knowledge or poor understanding of God's word. In 1 John 3:7-9 we see that Christians who are at risk of deception are spiritual children.

> *Dear children, don't let anyone deceive you about this: When people do what is right, it shows that they are righteous, even as Christ is righteous. 8 But when people keep on sinning,*

it shows that they belong to the devil, who has been sinning since the beginning. But the Son of God came to destroy the works of the devil. 9 Those who have been born into God's family do not make a practice of sinning, because God's life is in them. So they can't keep on sinning, because they are children of God.

Spiritual children struggle to remain in fellowship with Christ (verse 28).

John has advised the children to remain in fellowship with Christ suggesting that they are prone to 'drop out of fellowship'. Any Christian who struggles to maintain an active walk with God is thus a spiritual child.

Spiritual children are denominational.

This one may shock you so please read 1 Corinthians 3:1-5

Dear brothers and sisters, when I was with you I couldn't talk to you as I would to spiritual people. I had to talk as though you belonged to this world or as though you were infants in Christ. 2 I had to feed you with milk, not with solid food, because you weren't ready for anything stronger. And you still aren't ready, 3 for you are still controlled by your sinful nature. You are jealous of one another and quarrel with each other. Doesn't that prove you are controlled by your sinful nature?

Aren't you living like people of the world? 4 When one of you says, "I am a follower of Paul," and another says, "I follow Apollos," aren't you acting just like people of the world? 5 After all, who is Apollos? Who is Paul? We are only God's servants through whom you believed the Good News. Each of us did the work the Lord gave us.

Again we see that being controlled by the sinful nature is a characteristic of a spiritual child or infant which we have already looked at. What really interests me here is the specific subject matter that Paul focuses on. He refers to them as spiritual infants primarily because they quarrel and are jealous over who their leaders are. Some favoured Apollos and others favoured Paul. This tells us that when you promote your denomination or your leader over the body of Christ as a whole, you are a spiritual infant. Boasting about your denomination is a mark of spiritual infancy. Christians who derive their sense of identity from their denomination and church leaders are spiritual children. Paul himself said we are only God's servants through whom you believed, we just did the work God gave us to do. Remember Goal 1, Unity of faith?

In the same vein, we need to be careful about calling every pastor or leader your spiritual father. Consider the following scriptures: Matthew 23:8-12, 1 Corinthians 4:15 and 1 Timothy 1:2

"Don't let anyone call you 'Rabbi,' for you have

only one teacher, and all of you are equal as brothers and sisters. 9 And don't address anyone here on earth as 'Father,' for only God in heaven is your spiritual Father. 10 And don't let anyone call you 'Teacher,' for you have only one teacher, the Messiah. 11 The greatest among you must be a servant. 12 But those who exalt themselves will be humbled, and those who humble themselves will be exalted.

For even if you had ten thousand others to teach you about Christ, you have only one spiritual father. For I became your father in Christ Jesus when I preached the Good News to you.

I am writing to Timothy, my true son in the faith.(see also 2 Timothy 1:2 and Titus 1:4)

From the scriptures it seems that a person qualifies to occupy the position of a spiritual father who preached Jesus to you and led you to the Lord or who personally mentors you into Christian ministry.

So, a spiritual child is one who is still living in sin, self-centred and self-seeking, easily deceived, struggling to maintain fellowship with the Lord and passionately denominational.

YOUNG IN FAITH

These are the adolescents of the Christian world. They have grown beyond being children but they are not fully mature. Again, there is nothing wrong with being young in faith; the real issue is staying at this level longer than you should. These Christians occupy the middle ground between immaturity and maturity. So what are the characteristics of those who are young in faith? Using 1 John 2:12-20 and some other scriptures as a basis, we find the following characteristics:

Christians who are young in faith are strong (1 John 2:12-13)

The word translated strong there is the Greek word 'ischuros' which means amongst other things, forcible, boisterous, valiant. These Christians have zeal, passion and exuberance. Having zeal and passion is a good thing. Jesus Himself said passion for God's house will consume me (John 2:17).

Christians who are young in faith have the word of God living in their hearts. (1 John 2:14)

This means the word of God is alive in them. Hebrews 4:12 says:

> For the word of God is alive and powerful. It is sharper than the sharpest two-edged sword, cutting between soul and spirit, between joint and marrow. It exposes our innermost thoughts and desires.

When the word of God is alive in you, it means your

life is exposed to the word, allowing it access to your innermost thoughts and desires. You have learnt to examine your life and motives by the word of God. You have acquired the knowledge required to move onto maturity in your faith. Paul the Apostle used a well-known phrase, 'that I may know Him.' in Philippians 2:10. These Christians have also started to develop and exercise their faith in God through His word. They are also more likely to start taking on situations in their lives using God's word as a basis for prayer.

Christians who are young in faith have won their battle with the evil one.

This characteristic is a very important one to understand. The Bible tells us overwhelming victory is ours. (Romans 8:37) Thus in truth, the more mature we are in faith, the less we battle and the more we walk in the overwhelming victory that Jesus has already obtained for us. A young in faith Christian is still fighting and winning battles (which is good by the way!) but a more mature believer rests in the victory already obtained by Jesus.

Christians who are young in faith are still tempted by the lure of the world (1 John 2:15-17)

This is why John had to admonish them not to love the world nor the things in the world. The world has only three things to offer: craving to feel physical pleasure (usually sexually related), craving to have what it sees and pride in achievements and possessions. See how the Amplified version puts verses 15-17:

15 Do not love the world [of sin that opposes God and His precepts], nor the things that are in the world. If anyone loves the world, the love of the Father is not in him. 16 For all that is in the world—the lust and sensual craving of the flesh and the lust and longing of the eyes and the boastful pride of life [pretentious confidence in one's resources or in the stability of earthly things]—these do not come from the Father, but are from the world. 17 The world is passing away, and with it its lusts [the shameful pursuits and ungodly longings]; but the one who does the will of God and carries out His purposes lives forever.

So, a Christian who is young in faith is one who has a great zeal for God, has the word of God active in their hearts but still probably has an ongoing battle with lust or pride in some form.

MATURE IN FAITH

These are the mature believers. Interestingly, John had only one thing to say about mature believers in 1 John 2 and he repeated it for emphasis. In verses 13 and 14 he states:

I am writing to you who are mature in the

faith because you know Christ, who existed from the beginning.

That's it? The only characteristic of believers mature in faith is that they know Christ who existed from the beginning?

Before we examine this, let us first establish by inference, what a mature in faith believer looks like. Having studied what spiritual children and those young in faith look like, we can imply certain characteristics of believers who are mature in faith.

- Christians who are mature in faith are not living in sin.

- Christians who are mature in faith know the Father and also know the Christ.

- Christians who are mature in faith are not at risk of deception.

- Christians who are mature in faith are not struggling to remain in fellowship with the Lord.

- Christians who are mature in faith are not denominational.

- Christians who are mature in faith are strong in zeal.

- Christians who are mature in faith have the

word living in their hearts.

- Christians who are mature in faith walk in the overwhelming victory which Jesus obtained.

- Christians who are mature in faith are not tempted by the lure of this world.

Coming back to what John said, the mature in faith know the Christ who existed from the beginning. This suggests that there is a knowledge of Christ that you can have, which only focuses on the Christ that came to die for our sins and give us His Holy Spirit, but there is another knowledge which embraces the Christ who existed from the beginning. Philippians 2:1-16 will help us understand this. It's a long passage but we will engage in some Bible study to fully understand what it means to be a believer mature in faith.

> *Is there any encouragement from belonging to Christ? Any comfort from his love? Any fellowship together in the Spirit? Are your hearts tender and compassionate? 2 Then make me truly happy by agreeing wholeheartedly with each other, loving one another, and working together with one mind and purpose. 3 Don't be selfish; don't try to impress others. Be humble, thinking of others as better than yourselves. 4 Don't look out only for your own interests, but take an interest in others, too. 5 You must have the*

same attitude that Christ Jesus had. 6 Though he was God, he did not think of equality with God as something to cling to 7 Instead, he gave up his divine privileges; he took the humble position of a slave and was born as a human being. When he appeared in human form, 8 he humbled himself in obedience to God and died a criminal's death on a cross. 9 Therefore, God elevated him to the place of highest honour and gave him the name above all other names, 10 that at the name of Jesus every knee should bow, in heaven and on earth and under the earth, 11 and every tongue declare that Jesus Christ is Lord, to the glory of God the Father. 12 Dear friends, you always followed my instructions when I was with you. And now that I am away, it is even more important. Work hard to show the results of your salvation, obeying God with deep reverence and fear. 13 For God is working in you, giving you the desire and the power to do what pleases him. 14 Do everything without complaining and arguing, 15 so that no one can criticize you. Live clean, innocent lives as children of God, shining like bright lights in a world full of crooked and perverse people. 16 Hold firmly to the word of life; then, on the day of Christ's return, I will be proud that I did not run the race in vain and that my work was not useless.

In summary this passage is saying the following

things which we have already explained are present in a mature believer.

- Walk in agreement, love and unity.

- Don't be selfish, don't try to impress others, be humble.

- Have the attitude of Jesus who gave up His divine privileges and took up humility.

- Because of Christ's humility, God exalted Him.

- Walk in obedience now more than ever.

- Work hard to show the results of your salvation, walking in obedience and reverence.

- Depend on God to do what pleases Him.

- Do God's work without complaining and arguing.

- Live clean innocent lives shining as bright lights.

- Hold firmly to God's word.

Christ from the beginning gave up His divine privileges and though he was equal with God possessing divinity, He chose to humble Himself and become a mere mortal, a servant.

A Christian who is mature in faith is one who despite his or her status in church or society chooses to live a humble life with no airs or graces, walking in love, unity and agreement, living a clean innocent life, shining as a bright light for God, holding onto God's word in faith.

SOME OTHER CHARACTERISTICS OF A MATURE CHRISTIAN ARE:

The mature Christian is still pressing into God.

Philippians 3:12-15 says:

> *I don't mean to say that I have already achieved these things or that I have already reached perfection. But I press on to possess that perfection for which Christ Jesus first possessed me. 13 No, dear brothers and sisters, I have not achieved it, but I focus on this one thing: Forgetting the past and looking forward to what lies ahead, 14 I press on to reach the end of the race and receive the heavenly prize for which God, through Christ Jesus, is calling us.15 Let all who are spiritually mature agree on these things. If you disagree on some point, I believe God will make it plain to you.*

Paul is saying in this scripture that he had not arrived at perfection but he was pressing towards it and if indeed we are spiritually mature we would agree with him.

The mature Christian is able to understand the wisdom of God

1 Corinthians 2:1-7 says:

> When I first came to you, dear brothers and sisters, I didn't use lofty words and impressive wisdom to tell you God's secret plan. 2 For I decided that while I was with you I would forget everything except Jesus Christ, the one who was crucified. 3 I came to you in weakness—timid and trembling. 4 And my message and my preaching were very plain. Rather than using clever and persuasive speeches, I relied only on the power of the Holy Spirit. 5 I did this so you would trust not in human wisdom but in the power of God. 6 Yet when I am among mature believers, I do speak with words of wisdom, but not the kind of wisdom that belongs to this world or to the rulers of this world, who are soon forgotten. 7 No, the wisdom we speak of is the mystery of God—his plan that was previously hidden, even though he made it for our ultimate glory before the world began

Paul is saying here that before they were mature in faith, his preaching was very plain but when he is among mature believers, he speaks the wisdom of God.

The mature Christian has love as his motive for serving God

1 Corinthians 13:1-3 says:

If I could speak all the languages of earth and of angels, but didn't love others, I would only be a noisy gong or a clanging cymbal. 2 If I had the gift of prophecy, and if I understood all of God's secret plans and possessed all knowledge, and if I had such faith that I could move mountains, but didn't love others, I would be nothing. 3 If I gave everything I have to the poor and even sacrificed my body, I could boast about it; but if I didn't love others, I would have gained nothing.

Paul is saying here that whatever gifts or abilities you have, without love as your motive, you gain nothing. John 3:16 tells us that God so loved the world He gave His Son. God has love as His motive and a Christian who is mature would too.

Much as I like the traditional means of determining your level of spiritual development (Spiritual children, young and mature in faith) it has a few flaws if used as a tool to aid spiritual growth

- It assumes that everyone matures in everything at the same time. The truth is that while you may be growing in one area of your life you may be stunted in another.

- It does not allow you to identify specific areas of growth to focus on.

There is another way which we will discuss next.

PRACTICAL SPIRITUAL GROWTH

This is the means by which you can assess, plan and practice your spiritual development using the seven goals which we looked at in Ephesians 4:11-16 as the basis for spiritual growth. You work with each goal with a view to determine where you are, where you need to go and what you need to do to get to spiritual maturity in that goal.

For example, I could look at the goal called "mature in the Lord". I see that it has to do with speech and character. I assess my life and see that I appear to be doing well in speech and character except when someone cuts in front of me when I am driving. Something wells up in me and I start seething with rage, feel like saying swear words and then remember I am a Christian! I feel convicted in my heart so I resolve to grow in this area. I commit myself to the Lord in prayer asking for His help, look for relevant scriptures and then start consciously controlling my outbursts when driving. In time, I would have matured in that area and I can then focus on another.

Is it possible to grow in one area and not in another? Yes.

Is it possible to reach full maturity in one area and be a child in another? Unlikely as they are all connected. You can't grow fully in one area unless you are also growing in the others.

Table 1.0 helps us to see how both means of assessing your spiritual growth correspond to each other.

	Children	Young in faith	Mature in faith
Unity of faith	Denominational in thinking	Understands the body of Christ	Walking in understanding of the body of Christ!
Knowledge of God's Son	Ignorant	Has knowledge of God's promises	Walking in God's promises
Mature in the Lord	Living in sin	Battling with sin	Victory over sin
Standard of Christ	Just speaks in tongues	Led of the Spirit	Fullness of the Spirit
No longer children	Unstable in faith	Steady in faith	Doctrinally sound
Speak truth in love	Unforgiveness	Learning to forgive	Resolving conflict
Find your place, release your grace	Receiving ministry	Doing ministry	Fulfilling ministry

Table 1.0

Here are some scenarios to help us practically use what we have learnt so far.

SCENARIO 1

Uz just started a new job but has been having problems with his manager who is always accusing him of messing things up. He feels he has been doing his best but is now getting very frustrated. He has been taking his frustrations home and shouted at his daughter for no real reason. At work he is now regularly getting confrontational with his manager which is making things worse. What goals of spiritual growth come into play here?

Uz needs to grow in the goal, "Mature in the Lord". A Christian who is mature in the Lord in character, would walk in love and not keep his frustrations inside, and certainly not carry them home and take things out on his family. Uz needs to offload his frustrations in prayer to the Lord. Uz also needs to grow in the goal, "Speaking the truth in love" if he is wrongly accused. (It's another matter if this is arising because Uz is not doing his work to the expected standard). This will allow him to resolve things amicably and not continue to inflame the situation.

SCENARIO 2

Shan has been living in fear for the past 20 years of her life. Although she is now a Christian, she still remembers the word of her aunt who cursed her and told her she would never become anything significant in life and that she will die young. She has had a run of negative experiences recently and believes her aunt's curse is taking hold. She has attended countless deliverance prayer meetings and has had lots of ministers lay hands on her but she still has nightmares and also has difficulty sleeping. Some ministers have asked her for money to pray special prayers for her. What goals of spiritual growth come into play?

Shan needs to grow in the "Knowledge of God's Son". Jesus has already defeated the devil on our behalf so she does not need to live in fear. She needs to have faith in the finished work of Jesus and does not need to run from pillar to post seeking prayer. Until that happens, she needs to be discerning about who she goes to for prayer and whom she allows to lay hands on her and pray for her. That brings in the "Standard of Christ" and "No longer children".

SCENARIO 3

Zech has been a Christian for many years. God has been using him in the gifts of the Spirit and has been doing signs and wonders through him. He has had a few financial problems and he has decided that going into full time ministry to start a church would be a good idea. This will ensure he has a good income and he'll get to travel a lot and see places. His pastor has tried to discourage him but he told the pastor to stop being jealous of His anointing. What goals of spiritual growth come into play?

Zech and those around him need to understand that the fact that he has the gifts of the spirit does not make him a mature believer, just a gifted one. He needs to grow in the goal "Knowledge of God's Son" to help him understand the provision Jesus has secured for us with respect to his financial problems. He needs to grow in the goal "Speaking the truth in love" as he does not have love or the guidance of the Holy Spirit as his motive for starting a church and he was unable to accept the truth when spoken to him. He also needs to grow in the goal of 'Mature in the Lord' as he is likely to use the church funds for himself which is wrong and dishonest.

At this point I want you to identify the most pressing challenge of your life at the moment. An area of life in which you feel frustrated, unfulfilled, an area in which you keep falling down. What are the relevant goals of spiritual growth that you need to focus on to help you grow in that area?

In the next section we discuss how to grow from one spiritual level to another.

THE GATEWAY TO SPIRITUAL GROWTH

We have established what the goals of spiritual growth are. We have also established what the process is but how do we actually cross the line and start growing? What is the gateway we must cross that leads to spiritual growth?

Let us look at a couple of pointers in John 3:1-6.

There was a man named Nicodemus, a Jewish religious leader who was a Pharisee. 2 After dark one evening, he came to speak with Jesus. "Rabbi," he said, "we all know that God has sent you to teach us. Your miraculous signs are evidence that God is with you." 3 Jesus replied, "I tell you the truth, unless you are born again, you cannot see the Kingdom of God." 4 "What do you mean?" exclaimed Nicodemus. "How can an old man go back into his mother's womb and be born again?" 5 Jesus replied, "I assure you, no one can enter the Kingdom of God without being born of water and the Spirit. 6 Humans can reproduce only human life, but the Holy Spirit gives birth to spiritual life.

Jesus says in verse 3 that without being born again we cannot SEE the Kingdom of God. He then further explains in verse 5 that without being born of water and spirit we cannot ENTER the kingdom of God.

Let me first of all establish that the kingdom of God is not referring to the spiritual place we call, Heaven.

1 Corinthians 4:20 tells us:

For the Kingdom of God is not just a lot of talk; it is living by God's power

Romans 14:17 also says:

For the Kingdom of God is not a matter of what we eat or drink, but of living a life of goodness and peace and joy in the Holy Spirit.

The Kingdom of God referred to here is the life of goodness, peace and joy in the Holy Spirit, HERE ON EARTH! It is living by God's power here on earth! The Kingdom of God is literally Heaven on earth.

You SEE it when you get born again. Your eyes are open so you believe it, realise it is possible and you long for it BUT you only ENTER it, access it and start to enjoy it when you become acquainted or connected with the Holy Spirit! The Holy Spirit is the one who gives birth to spiritual life. The more of the Holy Spirit you allow in you, the more of the life of God you are allowing in you.

Jesus said what is born of flesh is flesh and what is born of Spirit is spirit. (John 3:6). Paul also says in 1 Corinthians 2:14:

But people who aren't spiritual can't receive these truths from God's Spirit. It all sounds

> *foolish to them and they can't understand it,*
> *for only those who are spiritual can understand*
> *what the Spirit means.*

So as long as we remain in the flesh, even though we are born again, we will be unable to receive the things of the Spirit of God. If we operate in the Spirit, live in the Spirit or walk in the Spirit, we are able to receive the things of the Spirit of God. Galatians 5:16-17 and Romans 8:5-9 put it very clearly.

> *So I say, let the Holy Spirit guide your lives.*
> *Then you won't be doing what your sinful*
> *nature craves. 17 The sinful nature wants*
> *to do evil, which is just the opposite of what*
> *the Spirit wants. And the Spirit gives us*
> *desires that are the opposite of what the sinful*
> *nature desires. These two forces are constantly*
> *fighting each other, so you are not free to carry*
> *out your good intentions.*

> *Those who are dominated by the sinful nature*
> *think about sinful things, but those who are*
> *controlled by the Holy Spirit think about*
> *things that please the Spirit. 6 So letting your*
> *sinful nature control your mind leads to death.*
> *But letting the Spirit control your mind leads*
> *to life and peace. 7 For the sinful nature is*
> *always hostile to God. It never did obey God's*
> *laws, and it never will. 8 That's why those*
> *who are still under the control of their sinful*
> *nature can never please God. 9 But you are*
> *not controlled by your sinful nature. You are*

controlled by the Spirit if you have the Spirit of
God living in you...

With the Holy Spirit guiding and controlling our lives, we won't be dominated by our sinful nature and we won't do what our sinful nature craves. We will instead, develop the right desires which lead to life, peace and mature Christian lives.

I have gone into all of that to explain the following:

- We came to salvation through Jesus by being born again

- However, just being born again is no guarantee of spiritual growth. You may know about it but not be able to enjoy it. It is possible to remain in the natural and not understand the things of the Spirit of God.

- We need to connect with the Holy Spirit to start enjoying spiritual things in general especially spiritual growth.

- The Holy Spirit is the Gateway to spiritual growth.

WALKING IN THE SPIRIT

If we need to connect with the Holy Spirit to enjoy spiritual things especially spiritual growth, how do we do that?

The Bible tells us in Galatians 5:16 to walk in the spirit so that we will not fulfil the lusts of the flesh. In other words, walk in the spirit and you will not walk in the flesh. So the question is 'How do we walk or operate in the spirit'?

The answer to that is found in Jude: 3-23. It is a fairly long passage but a very interesting read. I want you to read the passage so I have put it here instead of asking you to read it yourself.

Dear friends, I had been eagerly planning to write to you about the salvation we all share. But now I find that I must write about something else, urging you to defend the faith that God has entrusted once for all time to his holy people. 4 I say this because some ungodly people have wormed their way into your churches, saying that God's marvellous grace allows us to live immoral lives. The condemnation of such people was recorded long ago, for they have denied our only Master and Lord, Jesus Christ. 5 So I want to remind you, though you already know these things, that Jesus first rescued the nation of Israel from Egypt, but later he destroyed those who did not remain faithful. 6 And I remind you of the angels who did not stay within the limits of authority God gave them but left the place where they belonged. God has kept them securely chained in prisons of darkness, waiting for the great day of judgment. 7 And don't forget Sodom and Gomorrah and their neighbouring towns, which were filled with immorality and every kind of sexual perversion. Those cities were destroyed by fire and serve as a warning of the eternal fire of God's judgment. 8 In the same way, these people—who claim authority from their dreams—live immoral lives, defy authority, and scoff at supernatural beings. 9 But even Michael, one of the mightiest of the angels, did not dare accuse the devil of blasphemy, but simply said, "The Lord rebuke you!" (This took place when Michael was arguing with the devil about Moses' body.) 10 But these people scoff at things they do not understand. Like unthinking animals, they do whatever their instincts tell them, and so they bring about their own destruction. 11 What sorrow awaits them! For they follow in the footsteps of Cain, who killed his brother. Like Balaam, they deceive people for money. And like Korah, they perish in their rebellion. 12 When these people eat with you in your fellowship meals commemorating the Lord's love, they are like dangerous reefs that can shipwreck you. They are like shameless shepherds who care only for themselves. They are like clouds blowing over the land without giving any rain. They are like *trees in autumn that are doubly dead, for they bear no fruit and have been pulled up by the roots. 13 They are like wild waves of the sea, churning up the foam of their shameful deeds. They are like wandering stars, doomed forever to blackest darkness. 14 Enoch, who lived in the seventh generation after Adam, prophesied about these people. He said, "Listen! The Lord is coming with countless thousands of his holy ones 15 to execute judgment on the people of the world. He will convict every person of all the ungodly things they have done and for all the insults that ungodly sinners have spoken against him." 16 These people are grumblers and complainers, living only to satisfy their desires. They brag loudly about themselves, and they flatter others to get what they want. 17 But you, my dear friends, must remember what the apostles of our Lord Jesus Christ predicted. 18 They told you that in the last times there would be scoffers whose purpose in life is to satisfy their ungodly desires. 19 These people are the ones who are creating divisions among you. They follow their natural instincts because they do not have God's Spirit in them. 20 But you, dear friends, must build each other up in your most holy faith, pray in the power of the Holy Spirit, 21 and await the mercy of our Lord Jesus Christ, who will bring you eternal life. In this way, you will keep yourselves safe in God's love. 22 And you must show mercy to those whose faith is wavering.*

23 Rescue others by snatching them from the flames of judgment. Show mercy to still others, but do so with great caution, hating the sins that contaminate their lives.

The men mentioned in this passage must have been leaders of some kind as they had a level of influence. They must have experienced growth in some way but probably at some point in their Christian journey they missed it. Let's summarise the problems here:

- They did not grow in the goal no longer children in doctrine as they started to teach heresy (v4).

- They did not grow in the goal mature in the Lord as their character left a lot to be desired (v8-11).

- They did not grow in the goal find your place, release your grace as they had the wrong motives for service. (v12-13).

- They did not grow in the goal Standard of Christ as they were unfruitful, lacked grace and anointing. (v12-13).

- They did not grow in the goal speaking the truth in love as they were grumblers, complainers, braggers and flatterers (v16).

- They did not grow in the goal knowledge of God's son as they had to flatter and deceive rather than have faith in God (v16).

- They did not grow in the goal unity of the faith as they were creating division in the church. (v19).

These false teachers were operating in the flesh, sensual, causing divisions, not having the Spirit then the Bible says in verse 19 BUT YOU…! Meaning if you will be different, if you will not cause division, if you will not be a follower of the depraved natural instinct of the flesh, if you want to have the operations of the Holy Spirit in your life then these are the things you should be doing (v20-23). We see five things here:

- Build up your faith (v20).
- Pray in the power of the Holy Spirit (v20).
- Stay in the love of God (v21).
- Look for His mercy (v21).
- Reach out to others (v22-23).

These are what I call the Vital Signs of a Spiritually Growing believer or a believer who is walking in the Spirit. Just as you have Vital Signs in medicine, likewise these are the Vital Signs of a Spiritually Growing believer. When you check the vital signs of a person and they are good (temperature, blood pressure, pulse, respiratory rate, Glasgow Coma Scale or GCS), you are reassured that even if the person is ill, he probably has what it takes to recover without serious medical intervention.

Spiritually speaking, the presence of these signs indicate that you are spiritually alive and well and able to connect with the Holy Spirit who is the gateway for spiritual growth. The absence of these signs indicate that all is not well and it is likely you are not connecting effectively with the Holy Spirit which will probably result in defective spiritual growth.

BUILDING YOURSELVES ON YOUR MOST HOLY FAITH

This refers to the word of God which is the *cuisine* or food of the spirit. 1 Peter 2:2-3 says

> *Like new-born babies, you must crave pure spiritual milk so that you will grow into a full experience of salvation. Cry out for this nourishment, 3 now that you have had a taste of the Lord's kindness.*

The word of God feeds your spirit making it strong and healthy enough to connect with the Holy Spirit. 2 Timothy 3:16-17

> *All Scripture is inspired by God and is useful to teach us what is true and to make us realize what is wrong in our lives. It corrects us when we are wrong and teaches us to do what is right. 17 God uses it to prepare and equip his people to do every good work*

When a Christian is well fed with the food of God's word, his spirit is strong enough to receive whatever the Holy Spirit has for him.

PRAYING IN THE POWER OF THE HOLY SPIRIT

This is the *communication* of the spirit and does not only refer to praying in tongues. Any form of Spirit inspired prayer is praying in the power of the Holy Spirit. Ephesians 6:18 says,

> Pray in the Spirit at all times and on every occasion. Stay alert and be persistent in your prayers for all believers everywhere

Praying in the power of the Spirit on a regular basis opens you up to the leading and guidance of the Holy Spirit which makes you more available to connect with Him. It is easier to pray in the power of the Spirit when praying in tongues but it is also very easy to pray in tongues without focusing on the Holy Spirit.

KEEP YOURSELF IN THE LOVE OF GOD

Love is the *character* of the spirit and also the *commandment* of the Spirit as told us in 1 Corinthians 13:4-8 and John 13:34 below.

> Love suffers long and is kind; love does not envy; love does not parade itself, is not puffed up; 5 does not behave rudely, does not seek its own, is not provoked, thinks no evil; 6 does not rejoice in iniquity, but rejoices in the truth; 7 bears all things, believes all things, hopes all things, endures all things. 8 Love never fails. But whether there are prophecies,

they will fail; whether there are tongues, they will cease; whether there is knowledge, it will vanish away.

So now I am giving you a new commandment: Love each other. Just as I have loved you, you should love each other.

When you walk in love, you are operating on the same frequency as the Holy Spirit because God is love (1 John 4:7-8).

Love has boundaries; keep yourself safe there. That's where the Holy Spirit operates so He can reach you, keep you and help you grow to become more like Jesus. Love is a really deep concept. See what Ephesians 3:17-19 says about love:

Then Christ will make his home in your hearts as you trust in him. Your roots will grow down into God's love and keep you strong. 18 And may you have the power to understand, as all God's people should, how wide, how long, how high, and how deep his love is. 19 May you experience the love of Christ, though it is too great to understand fully. Then you will be made complete with all the fullness of life and power that comes from God.

This means that walking in love will make you and keep you strong, and will result in you being complete with all the fullness of life and power that comes from God. Isn't that awesome? This is certainly something we have not tapped into fully as the body of Christ. It starts to make sense that Jesus left us only one commandment; to love. This encompasses everything else. Walking in love will connect you to the Holy Spirit, opening your life up to all that God has to offer.

WAIT FOR THE MERCY OF THE LORD JESUS UNTO ETERNAL LIFE

This is the *comportment* or attitude of the Spirit. Psalm 123:2

> *We keep looking to the Lord our God for his*
> *mercy, just as servants keep their eyes on their*
> *master, as a slave girl watches her mistress for*
> *the slightest signal.*

Our comportment should be one of alertness, waiting for the slightest signal from the Holy Spirit. Although it originally means having our hearts set on the return of Jesus who will release us from mortality into immortality, it also means in a broader sense, being sensitive to the things of the spirit realm. When we are sensitive and responsive to Him, we are even more available to be led and trusted by God. He knows He can commit valuable things to us because we wait on Him, our spirits have a comportment of waiting on Him.

REACH OUT TO OTHERS

This is the *commission* of the spirit. We are not to live selfish, self-centred lives, we are to reach out to those who are less spiritually mature than we are and also to those who are living in sin taking care not to be stained with their spiritually filthy garments. We are to reach out to those who have struggles in the areas where we are strong. We are blessed to be a blessing. Jesus, in John 7:37-39, tells us about one of the roles of the Holy Spirit.

> *On the last day, the climax of the festival, Jesus stood and shouted to the crowds, "Anyone who is thirsty may come to me! 38 Anyone who believes in me may come and drink! For the Scriptures declare, 'Rivers of living water will flow from his heart.'" 39 (When he said "living water," he was speaking of the Spirit, who would be given to everyone believing in him. But the Spirit had not yet been given, because Jesus had not yet entered into his glory.)*

Out of you will flow rivers of living water. One of the main purposes of the Holy Spirit is to give you the power to be an effective witness for the Lord. This means winning souls but also includes representing and projecting Jesus in your own sphere of influence at school, work or in the community.

These are the *Vital Signs* of a spiritually growing believer who is connected to the Holy Spirit, our source of spiritual life. Remember they are all vital. If you check your life and you find one missing, then you may be an ailing Christian who is in need of spiritual resuscitation.

If that's what you find on your assessment, that's okay. It's not where you start from that matters; but where you end up. How will you use the information you have obtained to ensure you are perpetually connected with the Holy Spirit?

In summary, this short section has been about recognising the importance of the Holy Spirit as the gateway to spiritual growth.

We also saw that in order to ensure we are walking in the spirit and not in the flesh we need to be doing certain things which are the Vital Signs of a Spiritually Growing believer. They are:

- Build up your holy faith (cuisine of the spirit)

- Pray in the Holy Ghost (communication of the spirit)

- Stay in the love of God (character and commandment of the spirit)

- Look for His mercy (comportment or attitude of the spirit)

- Reach out to others (commission of the spirit).

This is a new one you must be saying. Geology of spiritual growth? What is that?

The Oxford dictionary defines geology as the science which deals with the study of the physical structure and substance of the earth, its history and the processes that act on it. In other words, geology refers to the environment that permits life to flourish on earth.

The geology of spiritual growth thus refers to understanding the environment that permits or encourages your spiritual life to flourish. The first three sections we looked at have been all about what you need to do in order to grow spiritually. This section is about how the spiritual environment you are in affects your spiritual growth.

Discussing the geology of spiritual growth is actually scriptural considering that Jesus talked about His church being built on a rock.

Now I say to you that you are Peter (which means 'rock'), and upon this rock I will build my church, and all the powers of hell will not conquer it. Matthew 16:18

Psalm 92:12-13 further explains the relevance and importance of being planted in God's house.

But the godly will flourish like palm trees and grow strong like the cedars of Lebanon. 13 For they are transplanted to the Lord's own house. They flourish in the courts of our God.

Together these scriptures tell us that the church is built on a rock and that we flourish when we are planted in the courts of our God. These scriptures make us realise something really important about spiritual growth: The environment in which you are planted as a Christian matters, and will definitely affect your spiritual growth.

As a Christian you should be planted in a church family where you can flourish and grow. Although spiritual growth is personal, the church environment you choose to be planted in, can aid or hinder your spiritual growth. In farming, not every crop does well on every soil. Likewise, not every believer can flourish in every church even when they are Bible-believing churches. When you add that to the biblical warning about false teachers springing up, then you realise that you must be very selective about where you worship.

So how should you determine where to worship? Are there any scriptural parameters to help us decide where to be planted?

Just as the right soil for a specific crop has to have certain characteristics in the right amounts, the church that will help you grow spiritually must have certain specific characteristics. Remember the geology of spiritual growth is not about whether one church is better than another, it's more about finding and being planted in the church that best encourages your spiritual growth. Every church should ensure it has the right environment that encourages its people to flourish and grow as believers but your responsibility is to determine which church is right for you.

There are at least seven things to consider before you join a church or to help you decide if your church is still fit for purpose. They are the seven things pastors will find useful as parameters to build on and pray into the churches they lead. They are the seven things that ultimately decide the spiritual environment of any church which will determine how well its people grow spiritually.

ONE: THE LEADING OF HOLY SPIRIT.

This is the ultimate determining factor in deciding where to worship or which church to belong to. No one knows you like the Holy Spirit. In fact, He knows everything about you. Psalm 139:7-18 gives us some insight into the breadth and scope of the knowledge the Holy Spirit has about us.

I can never escape from your Spirit! I can never get away from your presence! 8 If I go up to heaven, you are there; if I go down to the grave, you are there. 9 If I ride the wings of the morning, if I dwell by the farthest oceans,

10 even there your hand will guide me, and your strength will support me. 11 I could ask the darkness to hide me and the light around me to become night—12 but even in darkness I cannot hide from you. To you the night shines as bright as day. Darkness and light are the same to you. 13 You made all the delicate, inner parts of my body and knit me together in my mother's womb. 14 Thank you for making me so wonderfully complex! Your workmanship is marvellous—how well I know it. 15 You watched me as I was being formed in utter seclusion, as I was woven together in the dark of the womb. 16 You saw me before I was born. Every day of my life was recorded in your book. Every moment was laid outbefore a single day had passed. 17 How precious are your thoughts about me, O God. They cannot be numbered! 18 I can't even count them; they outnumber the grains of sand! And when I wake up, you are still with me!

This would be a good time to review the Purpose chapter of the book, the Decasections of Life available free on *www.decasections.org* or *woleolarinmoye. com*

The section on 'Where should I be?' emphasises the importance of your divine location, being where God wants you to be. It gives examples from the life of people like Adam, Abraham and Isaac who did not flourish until they were where God wanted them to be. The ultimate determining factor for which church to belong to, is where the Holy Spirit leads you to be. We read in Psalm 92 that we flourish when we are transplanted into the courts of our God. Where does God want you to be? Where has He designated that your gifts and abilities would be best developed and better deployed?

Thus, not everyone of us will find ourselves in a cosy church where everything is picture perfect. In fact, the Bible says Jesus learned obedience by the things He suffered (Hebrews 5:8); implying that you learn most in uncomfortable environments. This is an encouragement to some believers who find themselves in church environments that feel uncomfortable for whatever reason; if that is where the Lord wants you to be, that is where you will flourish, grow and become all that God wants you to be. Muscles are developed when put under strain and it may be that God is working on your character. Let me show you a scripture about Jesus that will interest you in Matthew 4:1.

Then Jesus was led by the Spirit into the wilderness to be tempted there by the devil.

Did you see that? Jesus was LED BY THE SPIRIT into the wilderness to be tempted of the devil. The Holy Spirit led Jesus into the wilderness for the purpose of Him being tempted. When He passed the test of being tempted, Luke 4:14 which explains the same story written from Luke's point of view, tells us He returned from the experience filled with the power of the Holy Spirit. Be where God wants you to be, doing what God wants you to do and you will grow spiritually and be filled with the power of the Holy Spirit.

No pastor or church leader should forcibly hold on to a person who does not believe they belong to that church; no matter how talented or anointed they are. The leading of the Holy Spirit supersedes everything in this respect. People will only flourish and grow if they are planted there. In fact, being in the wrong place can be very unproductive for you as an individual and for the congregation as a whole.

Reflection for pastors:

- How much of the Holy Spirit is in operation in your church or ministry?

- Do you encourage your members to walk in the Holy Spirit?

- Are the gifts of the Spirit as explained in 1 Corinthians 12 in operation in the church you pastor?

TWO: THE LOVE OF GOD

This is probably one of the most crucial elements that should be present in any church. You should feel loved in your church family. When Jesus was leaving, He prayed primarily for love and unity amongst His people. He gave us a new commandment in John 13:34-35.

So now I am giving you a new commandment: Love each other. Just as I have loved you, you should love each other. 35 Your love for one another will prove to the world that you are my disciples."

When a church family is not walking in love, you will see bitterness start to spring up. This is what the writer of Hebrews warned against in Hebrews 12:14-15

Work at living in peace with everyone, and work at living a holy life, for those who are not holy will not see the Lord. 15 Look after each other so that none of you fails to receive the grace of God. Watch out that no poisonous root of bitterness grows up to trouble you, corrupting many.

As we are working at living in peace and living a holy life, we are supposed to look after each other to ensure we do not fail to receive the grace of God; but also to watch out that no poisonous root of bitterness is allowed to spring up allowing many to be defiled. The Amplified translation states that:

See to it that no one falls short of God's grace; that no root of resentment springs up and causes trouble, and by it many be defiled. Hebrews 12:15

A church that does not work hard to avoid resentment or deal with roots of resentment or bitterness that have already sprung up, will eat itself up from the inside.

We face enough pressure from the enemy and society, we do not need the stress of having to fight each other. Resentment was springing up in the early church when there was murmuring over how food was being distributed in Acts 6:1-4.

> *But as the believers rapidly multiplied, there were rumblings of discontent. The Greek-speaking believers complained about the Hebrew-speaking believers, saying that their widows were being discriminated against in the daily distribution of food. 2 So the Twelve called a meeting of all the believers. They said, "We apostles should spend our time teaching the word of God, not running a food program. 3 And so, brothers, select seven men who are well respected and are full of the Spirit and wisdom. We will give them this responsibility. 4 Then we apostles can spend our time in prayer and teaching the word."*

From this passage you can see that even in the early church, there was rumbling of discontent and accusations of discrimination, but the apostles knew that it was important to deal with it and they did so decisively by appointing anointed leaders who had the trust of the people to manage the process. I repeat what we mentioned earlier for emphasis:

A church that does not work hard to avoid resentment or deal with roots of resentment or bitterness that have already sprung up will eat itself up from the inside.

The interesting thing from this passage was that the allocation of food was the cause of the problems. Yet the apostles, realising the importance of dealing with the rumblings appointed anointed leaders to deal with the matter. Leaders are very important in this process and this sets us up nicely for the next point.

Reflection for pastors:

- How much of the love of God is in operation in your church or ministry?

- Have you put processes in place to ensure the stamping out of bitterness or resentment that has sprung up for whatever reason?

- How can you encourage your congregation to walk in love?

THREE: THE LEADERSHIP OF THE CHURCH

The leaders of a congregation will go a long way to determine if the members of that congregation grow and flourish as believers for many reasons. The Bible has laid out certain personal characteristics of a good church leader in 1 Timothy 3:1-6.

This is a trustworthy saying: "If someone aspires to be an elder, he desires an honourable position." 2 So an elder must be a man whose life is above reproach. He must be faithful to his wife. He must exercise self-control, live wisely, and have a good reputation. He must enjoy having guests in his home, and he must be able to teach. 3 He must not be a heavy drinker or be violent. He must be gentle, not quarrelsome, and not love money. 4 He must manage his own family well, having children who respect and obey him. 5 For if a man cannot manage his own household, how can he take care of God's church? 6 An elder must not be a new believer, because he might become proud, and the devil would cause him to fall. 7 Also, people outside the church must speak well of him so that he will not be disgraced and fall into the devil's trap.

The leadership of a church is an integral part of its environment which will help or hinder the spiritual growth of its members. There are 12 qualities expected of a church leader from this scripture:

1. Lives above reproach (No one has anything negative to say about him).

2. Faithful to his wife (Good husband, not just absence of adultery).

3. Self-control (Walking in the fruit of the spirit).

4. Lives wisely (Exemplary living).

5. Good reputation (Past evidence of good deeds).

6. Enjoys having guests (Hospitable).

7. Able to teach (Good understanding of God's word and able to communicate it).

8. Not an alcoholic.

9. Gentle and not violent (verbally in quarrelling or physically in actual fighting).

10. Manages his family well (ideally a good family man).

11. Not a new believer (maturing believer to avoid pride).

12. Good reputation amongst unbelievers.

Every single one of those characteristics is important. Going through the list can you see any that can be exempted? If a church has leaders that do not have all these characteristics, then the spiritual environment of that church will be defective and can hamper the growth of its members. In the last point under love, we discussed the importance of leaders being able to quell the fires of resentment and discord. If a defective leader tries to take a stand on an issue, he could be looked upon as a hypocrite. He may choose, out of embarrassment at his own life, not to take a stand which will allow negative occurrences to fester.

I must mention at this point that in the church, leadership seems to be evolving differently from how it was originally intended. A church leader is meant to serve and minister to the people but today many leaders bully and lord it over their members expecting favours and wanting people to commit their lives to them the leader, rather than to Jesus Christ our Lord. Remember, Jesus said he that will be greatest in the kingdom must be the one who is as humble as a child (Matthew 18:1-4). Divine Jesus humbled Himself to the point of mortality in order to serve His purpose. What an example for us!

Reflection for pastors:

- Do you have the scriptural qualities to lead God's people?

- Do the leaders who work with you have the scriptural qualities to lead God's people?

- What can you do to ensure these qualities are present in your leadership team?

- What process do you have in place to appoint leaders in your church?

FOUR: THE LANGUAGE OF THE CHURCH

Every church has a doctrinal language it speaks which reflects its doctrinal position.

Different churches speak different doctrinal languages. You have some which refer to themselves as 'deliverance churches', as the main thrust of their message is deliverance. Others call themselves 'faith churches' or 'holiness churches' or even 'grace churches'. Although most to an extent will acknowledge the entire scripture, certain aspects are more emphasized than others based on the leader's personal beliefs or convictions. If you feel comfortable in a grace church but are attending a deliverance church, you might feel frustrated there. Therefore, it is important for you to know and consider the doctrinal language the church speaks.

The spoken language too is important. If you cannot understand what is being said, then you will not be able to receive the message when it is preached or communicate effectively with other members of the congregation; but of even greater importance is the doctrinal language.

Many multicultural churches do not encourage the speaking of traditional languages as this alienates visitors or even members from other places. If you want to reach a diverse community, then it is important to always speak a unifying language so that everyone can feel a sense of belonging.

Reflection for pastors:

- What doctrinal language does your church speak?

- What doctrinal language should your church be speaking?

- Is the membership of your church clear on what 'language' is being spoken? This refers to both doctrinal and actual language.

- How can you integrate people into the

doctrinal language you believe your church should be speaking?

FIVE: THE LOCATION OF THE CHURCH

The location of your church refers to its geographical position. If the church you attend is too far away, then you need to re-think your commitment there. You may like the church and feel comfortable there but if regular attendance is not practical then you may need to reconsider your commitment. Ideally, your church should not be more than a 30-minute journey to ensure commitment. It is difficult to be more than just a 'Sunday service goer' if getting to church is an ordeal in itself.

In this day and age of technology you have many people who 'belong' to churches as internet members. They view the services online and may even participate in the giving. The problem is you cannot connect; the leaders do not know you so you remain isolated as a believer which is not ideal. Unless you have temporarily relocated for work or other personal reasons and you will be returning shortly, it is usually preferable to attend a local church where you can be known by the leaders and other members and be a part of what is going on.

Reflection for pastors:

- Who are you sent to as a church?

- Are you located in the right environment to make an inpact?

- Are the transport links to your church good enough or do you need to do more? (provide buses etc.)

SIX: THE LATITUDE OF THE CHURCH

The word latitude can be defined as scope for freedom of action or thought. Thus the latitude of a church refers to the internal reach and scope of its operations. Your church should provide you with scope for freedom of action or thought. This means two things.

1. You should feel free to be all that God wants you to be. You should be able to express your gifts and graces in your local church. If you cannot, you will feel frustrated and out of place.

2. You should feel free to think about what is happening in your church and you should also feel free to ask questions about what direction your church is heading in.

When these two areas are present, the members of a church have increased confidence and trust in the leaders of their church. When leaders are autocratic and act as if they are above reproach, there is a lack of confidence in the leadership. In this case the leaders often have to be forceful and bullying to get things done rather than promoting an atmosphere of love. A good church should make you feel a strong sense of belonging and connection. A good church has a clear direction and focus so that members can understand where they fit in. Many churches have vision sharing meetings to help members have a clear understanding of where the church is headed.

Reflection for pastors:

- Does your church allow members to express their gifts and graces?

- Does your church encourage members to ask questions about church operations?

- How do you feel when this happens? Do you feel threatened?

SEVEN: THE LONGITUDE OF THE CHURCH

Longitude can be defined as the angular distance east or west on the earth's surface. Thus the longitude of a church refers to the external reach and scope of its operations. A good church has an outreach arm that goes beyond its usual focus and impacts the community. Belonging to a selfless church that reaches the community will make you feel a part of something larger than just the local church. Many churches have various charitable arms such as soup kitchens, mission trips and outreaches, medical missions, supporting leper colonies and much more. For many years my local church has provided Christmas hampers containing everything needed for a Christmas meal

Reflection for pastors:

- Does your church have an outreach arm that does charitable work?

- What opportunities are there for outreach in your community?

The environment in which you are planted as a Christian matters, and will definitely affect your spiritual growth.

This has been emphasised over and over again due to its importance. You must remember though that there is no perfect church. If there is one, it stops being perfect the moment you join because you are not perfect!

This means that apart from the first consideration (Leading of the Holy Spirit), the other points are more like prayer or action points which you want to see come to fruition in whichever church you feel led to be planted in. Pastors can use the reflection points as means of assessing where the church they pastor is with respect to where they should be.

CONCLUSION

Ecclesiastes 12:13-14

That's the whole story. Here now is my final conclusion: Fear God and obey his commands, for this is everyone's duty. 14 God will judge us for everything we do, including every secret thing, whether good or bad.

The Amplified version for this same passage says:

When all has been heard, the end of the matter is: fear God [worship Him with awe-filled reverence, knowing that He is almighty God] and keep His commandments, for this applies to every person. 14 For God will bring every act to judgment, every hidden and secret thing, whether it is good or evil.

The final conclusion is this: spiritual growth is everyone's duty. We need to fear and reverence God and keep His commandments. He wants us to be mature, fruit producing believers otherwise Jesus would not have said this in John 15:4-8, 16

Remain in me, and I will remain in you. For a branch cannot produce fruit if it is severed from the vine, and you cannot be fruitful unless you remain in me. 5 "Yes, I am the vine; you are the branches. Those who remain in me, and I in them, will produce much fruit. For apart from me you can do nothing. 6 Anyone who does not remain in me is thrown away like a useless branch and withers. Such branches are gathered into a pile to be burned. 7 But if you remain in me and my words remain in you, you may ask for anything you want, and it will be granted! 8 When you produce much fruit, you are my true disciples. This brings great glory to my Father.

16 You didn't choose me. I chose you. I appointed you to go and produce lasting fruit, so that the Father will give you whatever you ask for, using my name.

Only the mature produce fruit and only the very mature produce lasting fruit.

Don't just read this book once; read it again and again allowing the truths therein to sink into your spirit and renew your mind. Let the word come alive in you resulting in lasting change. We want you to cross that line from spiritual child, to young in faith, to mature in faith.

Our prayer is that these truths will edify you and encourage you in your journey to Christian maturity enabling you to produce lasting fruit for our Lord in Jesus name.

We wish you every blessing!

Other Book from Decasections.org

The Decasections of Life

Author: Wole Olarinmoye
ISBN-13: 978-1-908588-10-4
Format: Paperback, Pages: 168

Book information

Do you sometimes feel deficient in one or more areas of your life? Do you feel that there is more to life than you are currently experiencing? Have you ever wondered if there were certain boxes in your life you are not yet ticking? Are you aware that there are at least ten areas of your life which all need attention? Have you ever thought about how the different parts of your life link up?

Inside The Decasections of Life, Wole explains that real success is only achieved when you are successful in all ten areas of your life. He breaks down each area of life and asks insightful questions throughout the book that will provoke you to reflect on your life, setting you on the path to true success. Once you start reading The Decasections of Life, you will see life differently and start to grasp everything that belongs to you. You cannot be the same again!

Other Book from Decasections.org

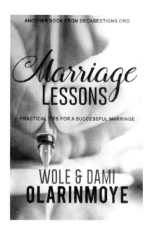

Marriage Lessons

Author: Wole & Dami Olarinmoye
ISBN-13: 978-1908588203
Format: Paperback, Pages: 104

Book information

'Marriage Lessons' is practical and outrightly down-to earth. In this thought-provoking and witty book, Wole and Dami Olarinmoye share valuable lessons from their personal experience of being 'single and seeking' and of the 'ups and sometimes not quite ups' of marriage. Single men and women will find useful tips for getting it right from the start and answers to some daunting situations. Finding the right partner is not enough; this book will help prepare you so that you yourself are Mr or Mrs Right.

Wole and Dami know how challenging marriage can be but yet show how exciting it can become once we learn to tango as a couple. They explore priceless themes which can tremendously enrich marriage like friendship and romance and, of course, sex. If you're bewildered by differences between you and your spouse, then you ought to read this book; it refocuses your mind on the beauty and complementary value of difference.

Other Book from Decasections.org

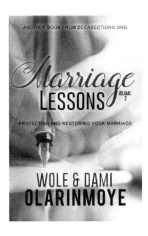

Marriage Lessons Volume2

Author: Wole & Dami Olarinmoye
ISBN-13: 978-1908588319
Format: Paperback, Pages: 112

Book information

What do you do when things are not working out as planned in your marriage? What could you have done to prevent this from happening? What can you do now that things have gone pear-shaped? You're set to get married, what can you do to ensure that unresolved issues don't threaten your marriage? In their second book on marriage, Wole and Dami answer all these questions and more. Marriage Lessons Volume 2 builds on Volume 1, delving into the detail of the most common problems in marriage such as, adultery, cross-cultural relationships, disparity in financial earnings, sexual incompatibility and more. They use several practical scenarios to help readers process and apply their learning. In addition, they introduce you their Marriage Health Questionnaire, a tool for picking up problems in marriages before they arise. Their 5 Ss tool also guides you through a practical, structured five-step sequence for resolving conflict in marriages. Prepare to be blessed!

Other Book from Decasections.org

The Garden Of Eden

Author: Wole Olarinmoye
ISBN-13: 9781908588326
Format: Paperback, Pages: 72

Book information

The Garden of Eden: the ultimate utopia, a place of peace and tranquility, paradise on earth. Have you ever thought about how idyllic life must have been in the Garden of Eden? Have you ever wondered what life would have been like if man did not fall into sin? Adam did not laze around Eden spending his days just plucking fruit from trees; he had an exciting, productive and fruitful life. In this book, Wole shows us that when Jesus redeemed us from the consequences of the fall, He restored us back to the Garden of Eden lifestyle. Several truths about the Garden of Eden lifestyle are directly applicable to us today as heirs of salvation. By applying these truths to our lives, we can enjoy the Garden of Eden life even today. It's a small book but it will change your perspective on life. Prepare to be blessed!

NOTES

NOTES

NOTES

NOTES